HOME DECORATING

HOME DECORATING

A WARD LOCK BOOK

First published in the UK 1995 by Ward Lock,
Wellington House, 125 Strand, London WC2R 0BB.

A Cassell Imprint

Copyright © Eaglemoss Publications Limited 1995
Based on The Country Look

Front cover picture: PWA International. Back cover picture: EWA.

All rights reserved. No part of this publication may be reproduced in any material form (including photocopying or storing it in any medium by electronic means and whether or not transiently or incidentally to some other use of this publication) without the written permission of the copyright owner, except in accordance with the provisions of the Copyright, Designs and Patents Act 1988 or under the terms of a licence issued by the Copyright Licensing Agency, 90 Tottenham Court Road, London W1P 9HE. Applications for the copyright owner's written permission to reproduce any part of this publication should be addressed to the publisher.

A British Library Cataloguing in Publication Data block for this book may be obtained from the British Library

ISBN 0 7063 7436 3
Printed and bound in Hong Kong

Contents

Painting techniques	7
Painting woodwork	11
Stencilled borders	15
Hanging wallpaper	19
Wallpaper borders	23
Wallpapering solutions	27
Tongue-and-groove panelling	29
Wooden floors	33
Laying a woodstrip floor	37
Sanding a wooden floor	41
Decorated wooden floors	45
Staining wood	49
Stripping wood	53
Reviving old furniture	57
Turn to stone	61
Tile style	67
Tiling a splashback	73
Simple shelving	77
Cupboard love	81
Wire-fronted cupboards	87
Introducing lighting	91
Index	95

Painting techniques

A room decorated in true cottage style should be simple and unsophisticated. A few coats of paint in fresh country colours on walls and woodwork are all you need, and act as the perfect foil for fabrics, pictures and rugs. Paint is cheaper than wallpaper and easy to apply with a roller or brush. It's not hard to achieve a professional finish, and highly satisfying results can be gained relatively quickly.

Choosing the paint
It's important to select the right paint for the job before you start, and this will depend on whether the paint needs to be washable and which type of finish you prefer.

Matt vinyl Suitable for interior walls and ceilings, this paint gives a smooth finish and helps to disguise uneven wall surfaces. It should not be used in kitchens or bathrooms where condensation may damage the finish.

Silk vinyl This paint has a low sheen which helps to reflect light. It is ideal for highlighting the relief pattern of textured wallpapers and plaster, and its waterproof finish means that it is suitable for kitchens and bathrooms.

Solid emulsion This paint comes in a paint tray ready to roll on to the wall. It is a good choice for beginners since it does not drip and is easy to use. Choose either the matt or silk variety depending on the finish required.

▲ *Good morning sunshine*
Sunny yellow paint on walls and woodwork is bright and cheerful.

How much to buy
Check the information given on the side of the tin or tray to check the covering capacity of each type of paint. Coverage will vary with the brand and the absorbency of the surface but, as a rough guide, 1 litre (2pt) of emulsion covers about 13sq m (15sq yd).

You can calculate the approximate area of wall surface to be painted by multiplying the width of each wall by its height and adding the totals for each wall together. Remember to double up if you're likely to need two coats.

◀ **Equipment**
From the top: roller tray with radiator roller and protective goggles inside; roller with long pile sleeve for matt paint; paint kettle; masking tape; wide paintbrush for large areas and narrow one for small ones or for edges; protective dust sheet.

▼ **Pretty in pink**
The mellow colours of a quilted bedspread have been used as the basis of this colour scheme. The walls and picture rail pick out the two pinks in the fabric, while the cream colour is used above the picture rail.

PREPARING SURFACES

For a good-looking, long-lasting finish, careful preparation is essential. Do not be tempted to skip this stage or you may have to re-paint sooner than you expect.

1 **Fill cracks and holes** Use a multi-purpose filler to fill holes caused by hooks, nails or screws and sand smooth when set.

2 **Wash all surfaces** Use sugar soap to wash the surface, then rinse off with clean water.

3 **Flaking or powdery walls** should be rubbed down and treated with stabilising solution. Treat newly plastered walls with emulsion thinned with water or an appropriate primer.

Painting with roller and tray or brush

Walls and ceilings can be painted rapidly with a roller which gives good, smooth results. However because it splatters a lot, you should cover carpets and any furniture nearby, and put on overalls or old clothes. The edges and small or awkward areas, such as above a curtain rail should be painted with a brush.

Materials

Paint roller Choose a medium size, 17.5-20cm (7-7¾in) wide, for ease of use, with a hollow handle into which you can insert a pole to extend its reach. The sleeves are made in either lamb's wool or a cheaper synthetic equivalent. Choose one with the right pile depth – long pile for matt or on textured surfaces, short pile for silk finish or solid emulsion paint.

Roller tray These are usually plastic, but you can get metal ones for really heavy use. They have a well at one end into which paint is poured, and a sloping, ribbed surface to remove excess paint from the roller sleeve.

Brushes If you don't want to bother with a roller and tray and don't mind taking longer with a large job, a 10cm (4in) brush is ideal for walls with a 2.5cm (1in) brush for the awkward bits.

Dust sheets Plastic dust sheets can be bought quite cheaply. Otherwise use old sheets to cover carpets and any furniture that cannot be removed.

Other useful equipment:

Goggles to protect your eyes when sanding and painting. They are particularly handy when painting the ceiling.

Radiator roller This is a mini roller on a long, angled handle which is used for painting behind fittings, such as radiators and pipes.

Paint kettle for transferring smaller quantities of paint from a large, heavy tin when you're using a brush.

Masking tape for protecting carpet edges, light fittings, glass, etc. If using on windows, make sure it doesn't get wet, or it will become very difficult to remove.

Step ladders Ideally get a pair so that a plank of wood placed between them will make a working platform from which to reach ceilings and high walls.

PAINTING A ROOM

1 Start at the top Prepare the surfaces for painting (see previous page). Work from the window end, starting with the ceiling.

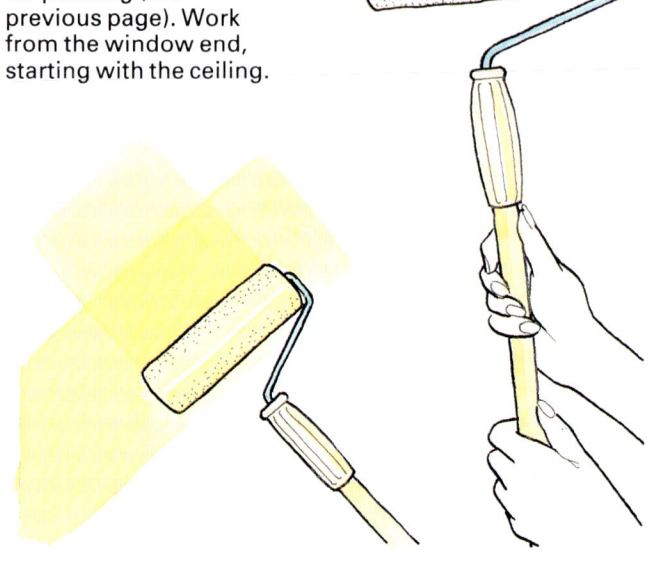

2 Painting with a roller Paint a narrow margin around the edges with a small brush. Load up with paint from the tray, running the roller back and forth over the ridges for even distribution. Wearing goggles to protect your eyes from splashes and with the roller fitted on an extension pole, roll the paint in criss-cross fashion across the ceiling, painting about 1m (1yd) wide strips at a time. Join up the strips quickly, before the wet edge dries, and aim to finish the ceiling in one go.

▲ **Come down**
A warm paint colour helps to bring down a high ceiling.

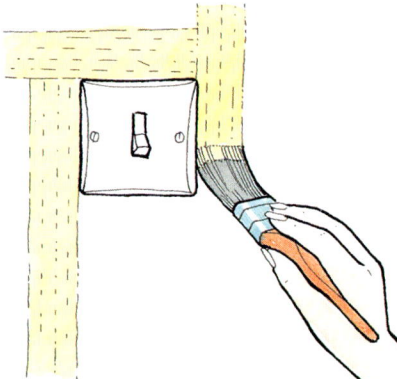

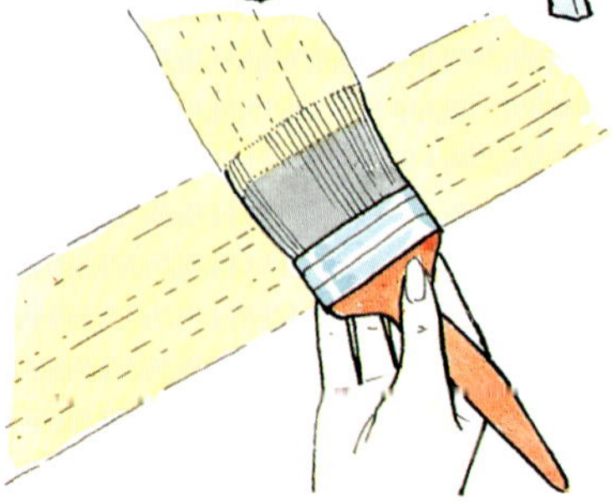

4 Painting the walls Use a narrow brush to paint along the edges of skirtings, window frames, doors and light switches first. Then paint with a roller or large brush, aiming to complete one wall at a time. Start at the top right-hand corner and work across in horizontal bands from top to bottom. Allow to dry thoroughly before applying a second coat.

---

tip

Successful storage
Sometimes, when you re-open a tin of paint you will find a thick skin has formed on the top which has to be cut out. Quickly inverting the tin before storing it seals the tin and prevents this skin forming.

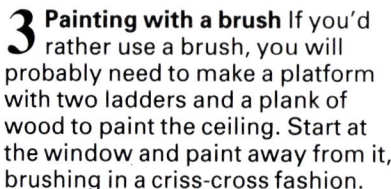

3 Painting with a brush If you'd rather use a brush, you will probably need to make a platform with two ladders and a plank of wood to paint the ceiling. Start at the window and paint away from it, brushing in a criss-cross fashion.

5 Cleaning up When you've finished work, wash the roller and brushes thoroughly, as instructed on the paint tin. The sleeves on rollers can be removed for easier cleaning. Store the brushes horizontally, and hang roller sleeves up.

Painting woodwork

Freshly painted woodwork gives a tired decorative scheme new life. Brilliant white is a traditional choice, but for a softer, country style, you could consider using one of the many tinted whites that are now available or a mellow pastel shade which compliments the other colours in the room.

Painting woodwork should be approached with care because the paint has a greater sheen than wall paint which means that irregularities show up more. For this reason surfaces should be very smooth and clean before you begin. Also paint splashes can be difficult to clean off because these paints are oil based, so you should avoid overloading the brush with paint as you work.

Having said all this, painting woodwork isn't difficult and it doesn't take long to paint a door, window frame or skirting. You don't need much in the way of materials either, which helps to keep costs down.

Paints for woodwork
Gloss with its highly polished finish stays looking clean and new for years. It is a very durable paint, making it ideal for windows and outside doors, and it is easy to clean and care for. It comes in liquid or non-drip form, although the slightly more expensive, non-drip gloss is best for the beginner. Liquid gloss needs an undercoat, whereas non-drip gloss can be used without one.

▲ *Blue link*
Cornflower blue gloss, used to pick out door knobs and mouldings, acts as a link with the blue china and compliments the warm yellow walls.

Satin or **silk** paints designed especially for wood have the subtle sheen of an antique finish which is perfect for the cottage look.
Eggshell is an oil-based paint which, when dry, has a satin sheen similar to satin and silk finish paints. More commonly used for walls, it is not as durable as the other wood paints, but it is ideal for broken colour work on wooden surfaces – sponging, rag-rolling and dragging, for example.

Other materials required

Brushes Natural hog's hair bristles give the best finish, but nylon is cheaper and easy to clean. You will need different sizes depending on what you wish to paint: 75mm (3in) for doors, 50mm (2in) for skirtings and 25mm (1in) for window frames. An angled, cutting-in brush is best for windows.

Glasspaper, **paint stripper** and **scraper** to remove old paint as necessary.

Masking tape to protect window panes and other surfaces from paint. Remove before the paint is fully dry.

Cleaning solution to clean brushes afterwards. Check the manufacturer's instructions on the tin – some paints can be cleaned off with washing-up liquid and warm water, while for others white spirit is required.

Protective clothing including overalls and gloves.

PREPARING WOODWORK

Good paintwork If the existing paintwork is in good condition, prepare it by sanding with glasspaper. Alternatively apply liquid sandpaper, which roughs up the surface enough to make a key for the new paint.

Flaking paint If the existing paintwork is basically in good condition, but with some flaking in one or two small areas, you may find it is sufficient just to scrape off the flaking paint and then sand down so that the surface blends into the remaining paintwork.

Rough surface If the existing paint is pitted from layer upon layer of old paint, or if it is split or flaking badly, it is necessary to strip off and start again. Use a hot air or chemical paint stripper, following the instructions carefully and using a scraper to get off the melted paint.
  Wear protective clothing including leather gloves if using a hot air stripper, or rubber gloves if using a chemical one. Treat the stripped wood as bare wood, sanding until smooth and then using primer.

Bare wood New wood or wood that has been exposed by stripping or sanding should be sanded smooth, starting with a rough glasspaper to remove the remains of any old paint, and finally smoothing with a fine grade glasspaper. Apply a coat of wood primer before painting.

◀ *Moody blue*
A pale colour paint, such as this moody blue, produces a very restful effect which is particularly suitable for bedrooms. The low sheen paint used here also adds to the mellow, low-key effect.

PAINTING A DOOR

Preparation Remove any door furniture and prepare the surface as described on the previous page. Wipe with a damp cloth to remove dust and wedge the door open while you paint. Bare wood should be given a coat of primer before it is painted. If using liquid gloss, you will also need an undercoat.

▲**Emphasizing shape**
The attractive shape of a panelled door is emphasized by using a darker colour – in this case a warm yellow – to pick out the panels and door frame. A pretty stencil is the finishing touch.

The door frame When the door is dry, paint the frame. If the door fits snugly do not build up too many layers on the inner edge of the frame or the door may not close. Do not paint the door hinges.

WIPING UP

The oil-based paints which are used for painting woodwork are more difficult to remove than the water-based emulsions used on walls. Splashes should be wiped up immediately, so keep a rag or cloth soaked in cleaning solution to wipe up splashes as they occur. Do not use tissue or kitchen paper for wiping, since these can leave fibres behind which may spoil the smooth look of the finished paintwork.

When you need to take a short break, there is no need to clean the brushes completely. Seal paint-laden brushes in air-tight polythene bags to keep them moist and ready for use.

Flush doors Paint the edge of the door first, then starting from the top, make long, smooth strokes, brushing in one direction. Without re-loading the brush, lightly brush across the paint to prevent brush marks and to remove drips. Lightly brush from the bottom of the door up, to finish.

Panelled doors Paint the edge of the door first, then starting from the top, paint the panels first, applying the paint in the same way as for a flush door. Then paint the vertical, centre bar, followed by the horizontal bars above, between and below the panels. Finally, finish with the side vertical strips.

PAINTING MOULDINGS

Narrow mouldings, such as picture rails or panelling, should be painted with a small brush, preferably a cutting-in brush which has an angled edge. For wide mouldings, such as skirtings or architrave, paint the edge with a small brush first, then fill in with a larger brush.

For skirtings, use a paint shield which not only keeps the floor clean, but prevents the dust under the skirting from getting on to the newly

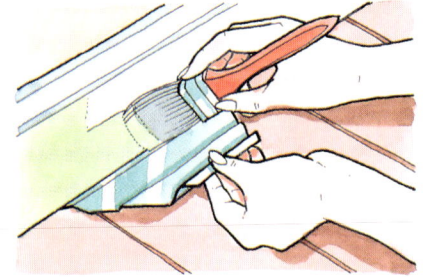

painted wood. A piece of clean, stiff card can be used as an improvised paint shield.

PAINTING WINDOWS

Preparation Prepare the wood for painting, then, unless you have a very steady hand, mask off the edge of the glass with masking tape. When painting the outside of a window, make sure the tape does not get wet from rain, or it may be difficult to remove later.

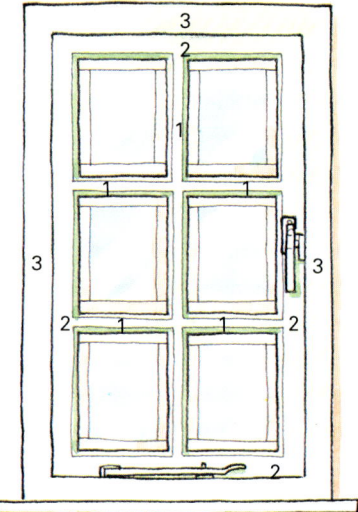

Order of work Using a narrow brush, or preferably a cutting-in brush which is angled for narrow areas, paint the horizontal and vertical glazing bars first. Then paint the rest of the window from the top down, and end with the frame. Remove any splashes from the glass while still wet, or use a razor blade to scrape away dry paint.

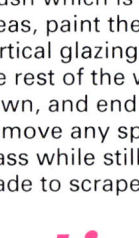

Paint seal
To seal any cracks between the wood and glass, place the masking tape 3mm (1/8in) away from the wood. This means that the paint will just overlap the glass, forming a seal. Do not paint primer or undercoat on glass as this will not hold.

◀ **Pretty and practical**
Banisters and skirtings should be painted in gloss since this is the most durable of the woodwork paints, and stands up well to knocks. A cutting-in brush will make painting the spindles a lot easier.

Stencilled borders

A stencilled room has a memorable 'handmade' charm of its own. In addition to the special decorative qualities of the actual painted motifs, continuous stencil designs – stencilled borders and friezes – can work 'architecturally', just like wallpaper borders. They can, for example, be used to enhance existing features such as fireplaces and arches, or they can make featureless interiors more interesting. In a room with expanses of plain wall, a stencilled frieze or panel can add character as well as subtly altering the space's proportions, making it feel cosier.

Borders can be continuous or non-continuous – either the stencil is designed to be repeated or one or more motif stencils are arranged as a border.

Continuous stencilled borders can be used as substitutes for absent picture and dado rails, helping to 'lower' the ceilings. Around doors and windows, a stencilled border frames and decorates in the same way as a wallpaper border

▲ **Fresh and fanciful**
The clean white paintwork and clear light shining through this casement window are underlined by a lightly stencilled two-colour floral border. In a small room, details such as these bring a pretty and individual touch to the room's decoration.

but with more subtlety. Any part of the stencil can be picked out and used as a motif on furniture or accessories.

Planning and measuring
Any large, repeat stencil design needs to be accurately measured and marked out. If you are stencilling a border all around a room, first decide on its position: for example, above or below a dado rail, at ceiling level or above a skirting board. These are useful linear features against which you can line up the top or bottom edge of the stencil.

If you have chosen a mid-way point, use a plumbline to find the vertical (see page 21), and a set square or a batten and spirit level to find the horizontal. Make your marks lightly in pencil or chalk along the length of the wall to provide a guideline. Calculate how many times you will need to repeat the stencil to reach each corner, not forgetting to include in your calculation any spaces between motifs.

To avoid an unnatural break in the stencil pattern at corners, you may need to alter the length of the spaces between repeat sections. This only works if the design is flowing and isn't meant to join up precisely.

Some stencils are made from plastic which is flexible and can be bent around the corner. You will need to hold the stencil firmly in your hand while you apply the paint – it will spring back if it is only secured with tape.

Because walls are rarely absolutely straight and the corners are hardly ever at true angles – even after the most painstaking planning – you often need to make final adjustments by eye.

WHERE TO START

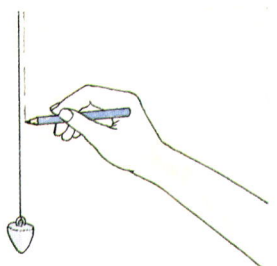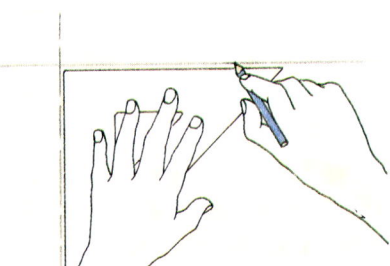

1 Marking the vertical Use a plumb line to find the true vertical and mark with chalk or pencil, which can be rubbed out after stencilling.

2 Marking the horizontal Using a set square, mark a horizontal line at right angles to the vertical line.

STENCILLING A CONTINUOUS BORDER

1 Preparation First assemble all the tools and materials you need and make sure the wall surface is clean, smooth and dry.

3 Preparing to paint Stir the paint and pour a small amount into a foil or plastic tray. Dampen sponge and wring dry before dipping it lightly into the paint and then dabbing against kitchen paper until the sponge seems virtually dry.

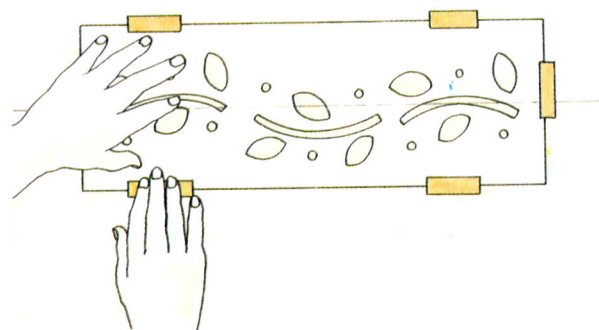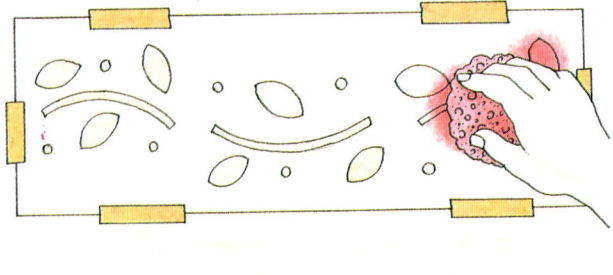

2 Positioning the stencil Mark the centre point of the wall, at the required height, lightly in pencil. Place the centre of the stencil on this mark and secure all round the outer edges with masking tape.

4 Applying paint Work from the outer edges inwards, pressing lightly. Don't worry if the impression seems very faint. It is better to build up colour gradually than all at one go. Too much paint on the sponge will only lead to smudging around the cut edges and seeping through on the underside.

◀▼▶ **Positioning a stencil**
To break up an expanse of plain wall, stencil a charming border at dado level (left) – about 90cm (3ft) from the floor.

The blue and green floral garland (below) is stencilled in place of a skirting board on this rough, white plaster wall.

A trailing design is used to give some definition to the plain plastered walls (right). This sort of ceiling-height stencil is perfect for bedrooms and bathrooms, giving intimacy and warmth.

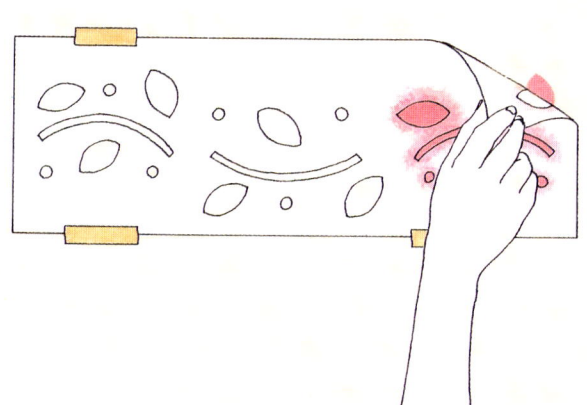

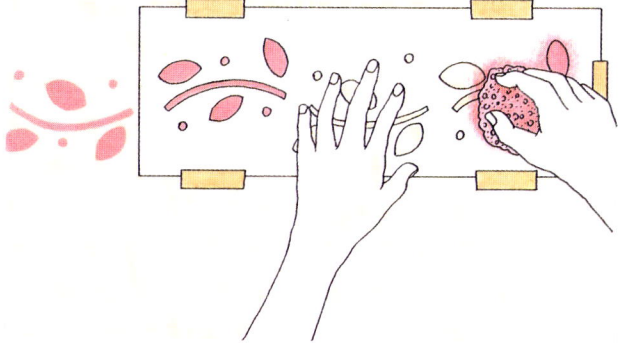

5 Monitoring progress Carefully lift up the stencil at one corner to check the results, and, when you are satisfied, peel it off, keeping the tape intact. There is no need to re-apply it as you move around the room.

6 Continuing the design Re-align the stencil for the next position. Work away from the centre of the design towards the corners. If using one colour only, continue all round the room.

Multi-colour stencils Where two or more colours are involved, complete the first and allow it to dry before returning to the starting point to stencil the next colour. Some stencils offer one sheet for each colour. For others you will need to mask out the areas already painted in, with masking tape.

A NON-CONTINUOUS BORDER

Organizing the repeats Take each wall separately and calculate how many times the stencil will fit into the space. The spacing between the motifs should be consistent.

▼ **Decorative arch** Floral motifs have been carefully planned to create a border around this hall arch. In the hall beyond, a border stencil has been used at ceiling level.

Variations in colour
Experiment with different applicators to vary the appearance of the colour. Natural sponges give a stippled effect, paint pads a more matt base colour, while small rags, crumpled up into a ball and dipped in paint create a water-marked look.

STENCILLING RIGHT ANGLES

For a stencilled border around a door or window you will need to pivot the design at the corners.

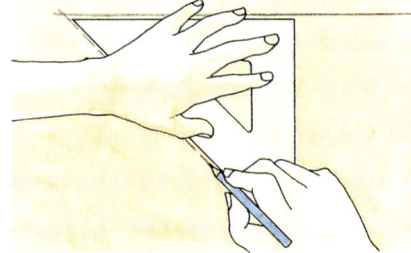

1 Mitring geometric designs To give a professional finish corners have to be mitred. Mark a horizontal line as before. Using a set square, draw a line at a 45° angle to cross it. Place masking tape along this line.

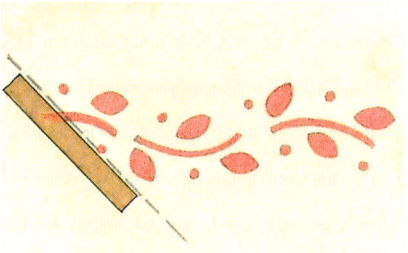

2 Applying the paint Stencil along the horizontal line, taking the paint over the edge of the masking tape. Remove the stencil and the tape and leave the motif until dry.

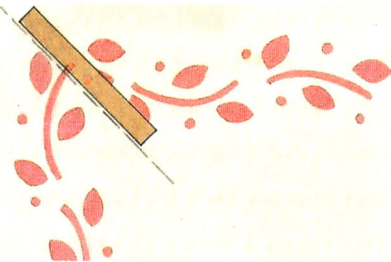

3 The vertical stencil Re-position the tape along the other side of the diagonal line, over the completed dry paint. Repeat as before. When dry, rub out the pencilled line.

Butting corners With simple, evenly-spaced designs, simply work out the best point to break off at a corner and start the vertical section directly beneath it.

Trailing corners With a flowing, floral type of design, it is possible to make it curve gently around a corner. Try a few experiments on test paper first. Start by printing the horizontal section, making sure it ends at a point where it looks complete. Turn the stencil at right angles and make the link with the vertical border by omitting or adding a few design elements.

Hanging wallpaper

▲ **Difficult corners** *Floral wallpapers suit the cosiness of this attic bedroom. The walls are papered in an all-over small floral paper, with a complementary sprig pattern on the ceiling. Note how the two papers are clearly separated with a cornice in an accent colour.*

A fresh patterned wallpaper can bring a room to life, with the added advantage that an all-over pattern helps disguise imperfections. For the most satisfying effects, wallpapering requires planning and attention to detail. (If you haven't wallpapered before, gain confidence by starting with a small room.)

This chapter deals with squared-up walls in good condition. Pages 23–26 show how to hang wallpaper borders, and pages 27–28 explain how to cope with switches, sockets, doors and windows.

Preparing the surface

The surface to be decorated should be as clean and smooth as possible. Usually, it is best to remove old wallpaper but if you know that the plaster underneath is in poor condition, and the existing wallpaper is plain, you could leave it in place to serve as a lining paper.

If you intend wallpapering on to new plaster, you must first brush on size. This is a watered-down adhesive which seals the fresh plaster and provides 'slip' so that the wallpaper can slide into position more easily. Sizing can be done days or hours before papering.

Choosing wallpaper

Don't be tempted to buy inexpensive wallpaper – a mediumweight quality is best because thin, cheap papers absorb the paste and stretch and tear too easily.

For a first attempt, avoid flock wallcoverings, which have fibres attached to parts of the pattern, and fabric wallcoverings such as hessian or silk. Relief wallcoverings, such as anaglypta, need care when smoothing into place and painting after hanging.

Measuring up

Before buying the wallpaper, measure the area to be covered. First, measure the height of the room from the floor or skirting board to cornice or ceiling – this is the length or 'drop'. Then measure the distance around the walls. Don't deduct the space taken up by doors and windows. With the two figures you can use the charts to calculate the number of rolls. Buy all the paper you need at the same time and check that all the rolls have the same batch number as the colour may vary slightly between batches.

If your paper has a large pattern, check it for the depth of the pattern repeat. If the repeat is, for example, 30cm (12in), then you need to multiply 30cm by the number of drops you need. If this comes to more than 10m (33ft) you will need to add an extra roll of paper to the total.

How many rolls?

Use the charts to calculate the number of rolls needed. The standard roll of wallpaper is 10m (33ft) long by 53cm (21in) wide.

Wallpaper calculator

The following charts are designed to help you calculate how many rolls of wallpaper are needed to cover a room.

METRIC — Wall height from skirting in metres

2–2.2	2.2–2.4	2.4–2.6	2.6–2.8	2.8–3	3–3.2	3.2–3.4	
5	5	5	6	6	6	7	10m
5	5	6	6	7	7	7	11m
5	6	6	7	7	8	8	12m
6	6	7	7	8	8	9	13m
6	7	7	8	8	9	9	14m
7	7	8	8	9	10	10	15m
7	8	8	9	9	10	11	16m
7	8	9	9	10	11	11	17m
8	9	9	10	11	11	12	18m
8	9	10	11	11	12	13	19m
9	10	10	11	12	13	13	20m
9	10	11	12	12	13	14	21m
10	10	11	12	13	14	15	22m

▲ Measurement round room in metres (including doors and windows)

IMPERIAL — Wall height from skirting in feet

6'6"–7'2"	7'2"–7'10"	7'10"–8'6"	8'6"–9'2"	9'2"–9'10"	9'10"–10'6"	10'6"–11'2"	
5	5	5	6	6	6	7	33'
5	5	6	6	7	7	7	36'
5	6	6	7	7	8	8	39'
6	6	7	7	8	8	9	43'
6	7	7	8	8	9	9	46'
7	7	8	8	9	10	10	49'
7	8	8	9	9	10	11	52'
7	8	9	9	10	11	11	56'
8	9	9	10	11	11	12	59'
8	9	10	11	11	12	13	62'
9	10	10	11	12	13	13	66'
9	10	11	12	12	13	14	69'
10	10	11	12	13	14	15	72'

▲ Measurement round room in feet (including doors and windows)

Newly hung paper
When you have just finished wallpapering, it may look unattractively blistered and patchy. But the irregularities smooth out as the wallpaper dries and after a day it will be flat and wrinkle free.

▶ **Wallpaper medley** A carefully positioned large floral border bridges the gap between the busy mini-print above and the cool stripes below. The wallpapers are hung first and then the border covers the join.

WHERE TO START

The first drop Nearly all modern wallpapers are designed so that the drops simply butt up against each other rather than overlapping; this means you can start to hang paper virtually anywhere in a room. Still, there is something to be said for the traditional technique of starting alongside the largest window and working away from it. Any shadows cast at the joins won't show because you will be working away from the light source. When using a wallpaper with a large, bold pattern, the first drop should be centred on a focal point in the room, such as a chimney breast. Subsequent drops are hung working outwards in both directions.

Use a plumbline This is a weight tied to a piece of string that is stuck to the top of the wall with masking tape. Pencil a vertical line down the wall against which the first drop will be hung. This will ensure the first drop hangs absolutely straight.

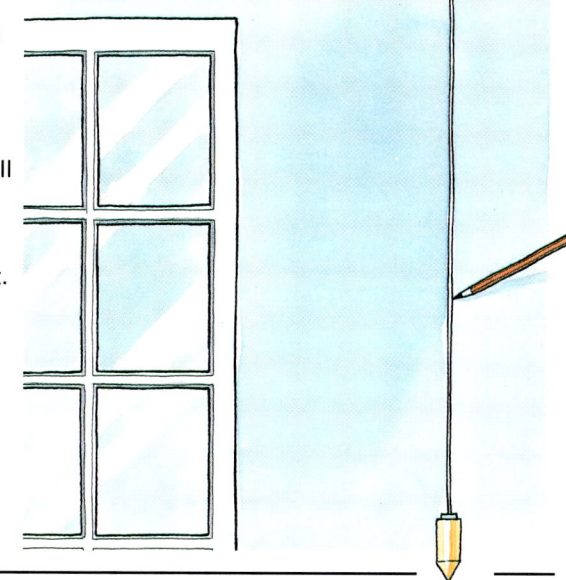

PAPERING WALLS

1 Measure the drop When you have decided on your starting point, measure for length, adding 10cm (4in) to allow for trimming at the top and bottom. This measurement can be used for all the full lengths of paper. Lay wallpaper face up on the pasting table and measure out the first length. Decide where the pattern will be placed. If the paper has a dominant print, make sure that a full pattern repeat is at the top of the wall where it is most obvious.

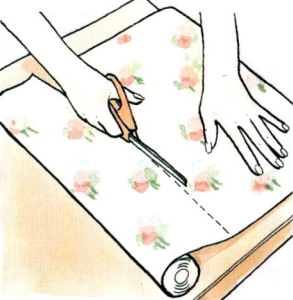

2 Cutting the drop Mark the cutting line in light pencil across the paper, check that it is at right angles to the edges, and cut along the line.

3 Match the pattern Now check the next length against this one to match the pattern before cutting. Mark the top of each length on the wrong side to avoid hanging patterns upside down and number as you cut.

4 Pasting the paper Lay the first length face down on the pasting table. Align the top and the far edge with the edges of the table, allowing the paper to overlap the table slightly. This prevents paste getting all over the table and on to the next length. Start pasting from the centre, working outwards and away from you, spreading the paste evenly right out to the far edges.

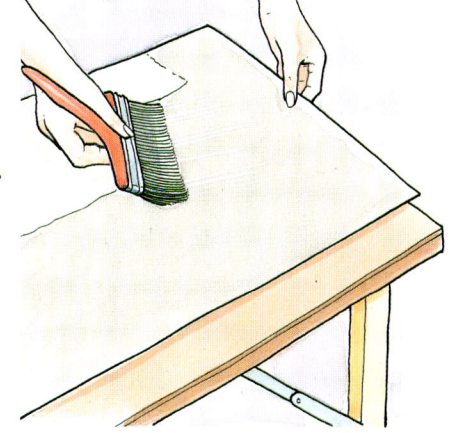

5 Paste the other half Move the length towards you, this time overlapping on the near edge of the table and paste the rest of the wallpaper.

6 Folding the paper Fold the paper up concertina fashion as you paste. Move the folded section along the table and paste the rest of the paper, continuing to fold in the same way. Some papers must be left for a few minutes for the paste to soak in or they will wrinkle when hung – follow the instructions on the roll label. Lay this folded paper to one side and paste the next length in the meantime.

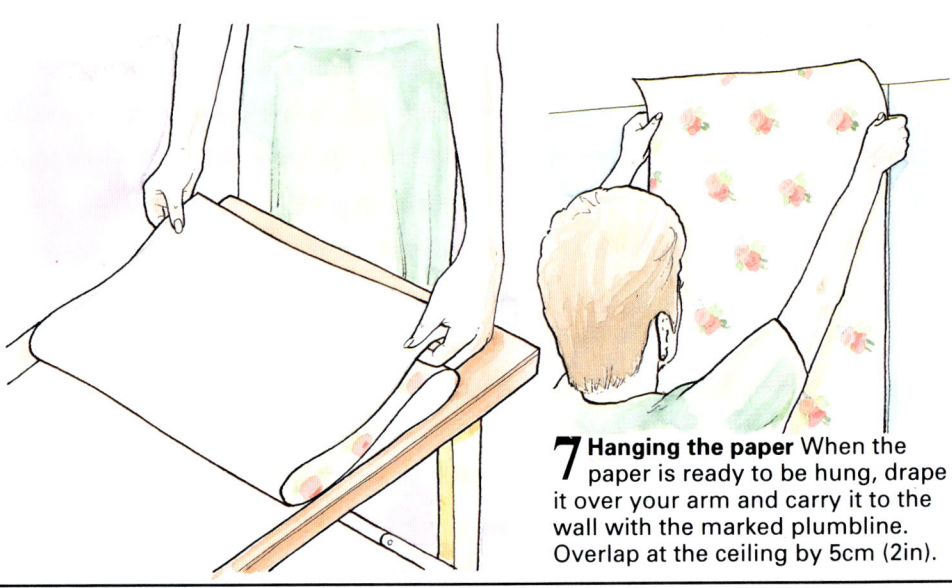

7 Hanging the paper When the paper is ready to be hung, drape it over your arm and carry it to the wall with the marked plumbline. Overlap at the ceiling by 5cm (2in).

9 Finishing off With a pair of scissors, make a crease at the ceiling angle and pull the paper back from the wall to cut along this crease. Dab the end of the paper back into place. If necessary add a little extra paste to the top edge first. Repeat this at the floor or skirting board and brush the paper back on to the wall. Remove any paste from the ceiling or woodwork with a damp sponge.

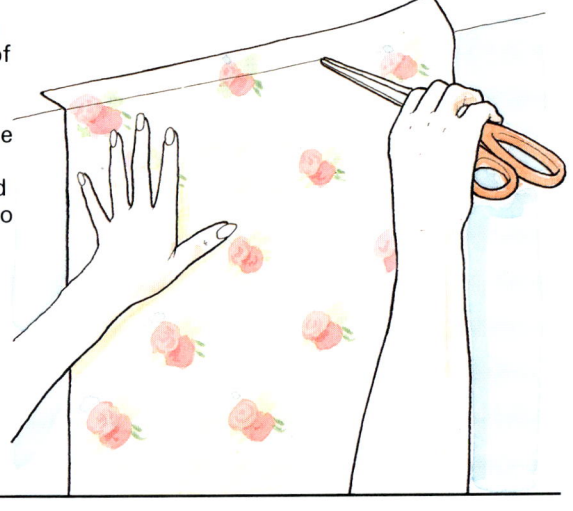

8 Removing air bubbles Unfold the remainder of the paper and working from the centre brush it on to the wall, removing any air bubbles as you brush.

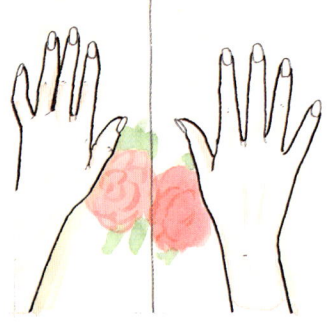

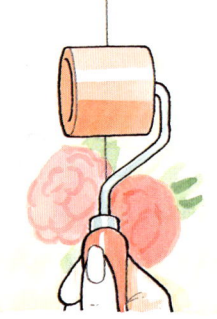

10 The next drop Paste and hang the next drop as numbered, matching the pattern exactly. To do this, slide the paper up or down using the palms of your hands. Brush into place and trim as before.

11 For a perfect finish Run a seam roller over the join about 20 minutes after hanging. Do not roll embossed papers – dab the seams firmly

12 Turning a corner Measure the distance from the last drop of paper to the corner. For internal corners, add 12mm (½in) to this measurement; for external corners, such as round a chimney breast, add 4cm (1½in). Cut a length of paper to this width and hang it with the cut edge brushed into (or around) the corner. Measure the width of the remainder of the paper and then measure this distance from the corner. Hang a plumbline from this point and mark the wall with pencil. Paste and hang the paper to this line, overlapping the amount carried round – any slight mismatch should not show.

Wallpaper borders

Wallpaper borders have an assured place in a country-style home. They can be used to emphasize traditional architectural features such as cornices, covings, picture and dado rails, or – in modern or renovated houses – they can substitute where there are none.

A pretty floral border around the room just below ceiling level will soften the contours of even the most featureless modern room. Borders can be applied over almost any sound surface with the exception of heavily embossed wallpapers and textured plaster such as Artex. They can be used on top of wallpaper, including low-relief woodchip papers (although here the results will be less perfect), or on painted walls and woodwork. You can even use them on painted furniture to give it a co-ordinated look.

Borders are also a quick and simple way of introducing a splash of pattern and colour into a plain room. So for maximum impact with minimum effort and expenditure, just study the simple step-by-step guide on the following pages.

Self adhesive borders are available in some ranges. With these borders you can dispense with paste.

▲ **Introducing flowers** *A wide floral border used at both picture rail and dado rail level brings a hint of the cottage rose garden into a hallway.*

WHERE TO PUT BORDERS

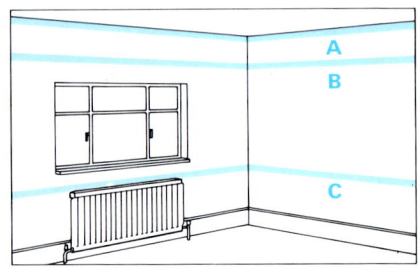

Just below ceiling level A border at the top of the wall finishes a wall neatly. It sits below the coving or cornice (if present) or butts up against the ceiling.

Picture-rail level In pre-1940s houses there was usually a picture rail – a wooden moulding fixed 30-45cm (12-18in) down from the ceiling. Many have been removed, which can leave a room looking badly proportioned since they helped to 'reduce' its height.

Dado-rail height A dado rail was often used by Victorians to prevent chairs from knocking against their costly wallcoverings. Also, the rail could cover the join between the fragile and expensive paper or fabric above, and a more hardwearing painted surface, such as anaglypta, below. The usual height was 90cm (3ft) from the floor – a third of the way between floor and picture rail.

Border placements A dado rail can be simulated by a wallpaper border (above), creating two separate areas for decoration. A picture rail border (below) is used to link two contrasting walpapers. Notice how the cornice has been picked out in a stronger colour to add definition to the decor. The ceiling border (left), positioned just below the cornice, co-ordinates with the floral motif of the bed linen and curtains.

Preparing to paste

The special **paste** used for borders contains more adhesive than ordinary wallpaper paste. Border pastes are sold in tubes for small jobs and tubs for bigger jobs.

An **ordinary paint brush** is used to apply the paste: use a brush that is about the same width as the border.

A **pasting table** or kitchen table, ideally 1.5m (5ft) long, will make your work easier.

You will also need a pair of **scissors**, a **paperhanger's brush** and a **seam roller** (optional).

Self-adhesive borders make the work even simpler. Lay them lightly in place and when you are happy with the result, press them firmly against the wall. They cannot then be moved.

How many rolls?

Most borders are sold in rolls 10m (11yd) long and in a range of widths from 21mm (1in) to 240mm (9½in). Around 50-90mm (2-3 in) is a useful size for most purposes – it is wide enough to show if used along the top of the wall in an average 2.5m (8½ft) high room, but not overwhelming.

To work out how many rolls you need to run a border around the top of a room, simply measure the long wall and the short wall and work out the combined length of all four. The measurements for a border at dado rail level, or at skirting board level are just the same.

If you intend to run the border around a door, or a window as well, you will have to measure them and add that to your total.

When you have the total length, round up the figure to the nearest whole roll. Allow a reasonable margin for error – if your sum works out to exactly five rolls, you should buy six as you will undoubtedly waste some.

Preparing the surface

Make sure the wall surface is smooth, clean and dry. If you are applying a border to freshly hung wallpaper you should leave it for at least 48 hours before hanging the border.

Establishing a guideline

It is difficult to get a border straight by eye alone, so draw a guideline in pencil to lay the border against.

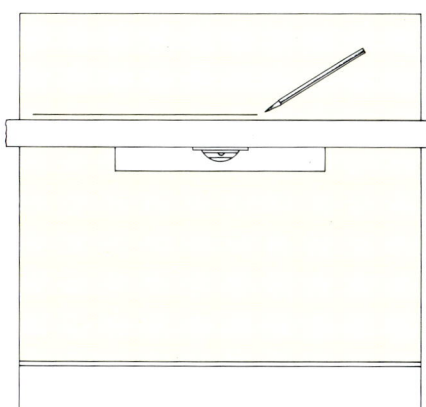

To draw a straight line against which to place the border, you will need a spirit level, a pencil and a long wooden batten.

Place a spirit level just below the height you want the border and rest a long batten on the top. Hold the batten in one hand and draw a pencil line along it to extend the spirit level line.

If you don't have a spirit level, mark the distance from the floor or ceiling at intervals along the wall. Then join up these points using a faint pencil line. This method is necessary if you are continuing the border up a stairway.

HANGING A BORDER

Hanging borders is easiest when you are laying the border against an existing feature – a coving or picture rail, for example.

If you are laying your first border around the top of a room, simply align it against the ceiling. Unfortunately walls are rarely straight, so in practice you will have to use your judgement and rely on your eye. In fact these imperfections will not show.

Often the junction of the wall and ceiling isn't perfectly straight. If the border doesn't butt up against the ceiling all along its length, fill in any spaces with paint that is the same colour as the ceiling. Use a small brush and a steady hand.

1 Unwind a sufficient length of paper to cover one wall but, before you cut it to length, hold it up and check that you have got the best positions at the corners. If possible, try to avoid cutting motifs. If you do have to cut a motif you will find that some cuts look better than others. Cut the length you require, allowing a small overlap (12mm/½in) at either end.

2 Lay the border face down on the pasting table and apply a strip of paste down the centre of the reverse side. Use the paint brush to feather the paste out to the edges, ensuring that the whole area is evenly and liberally covered.

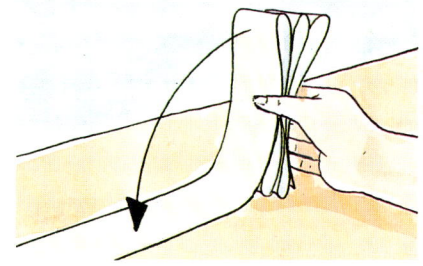

3 Fold the border up concertina-fashion, with the pasted sides together, so that you can hold it in one hand. With a long run you will have to repeat this process several times to get the whole length pasted. Wipe the table before pasting the next strip.

4 If you are right-handed, hold the concertina of paper in your left hand and work from right to left. This leaves your right hand free to work. Using your line as a guide (or the edge you are working up to), unfold a length of border, lay it on to the wall and press it lightly into place with the flat of your hand. Smooth it down firmly with a paperhanger's brush, working from the centre to the outer edges to expel air bubbles. Wipe off any paste.

5 Continue in this way along one side of the room. Take the paper around the corner on the first side. On the second side start with a slight overlap, adjusting and trimming if necessary so that you get the best pattern match. If you have one, roll the seam with a seam roller to get a good, flat seal.

Mitring corners

A well-mitred corner around a window, door or panel finishes off a job neatly. This is especially important where you have vertical stripes meeting horizontal stripes. Once mastered, the craft of mitring has many applications, increasing the decorative possibilities of borders. They can be used to outline mirrors, for example, or they can break up a large area of wall by creating 'panels'.

▶ **A narrow border** This has been used to create rectangular wall 'panels' on the plain coloured walls and to frame the mirror.

tip Disguising corners

With some borders, you can buy special decorative corner motifs to disguise corners. Alternatively, cut a motif from the border and paste it over the corner.

HOW TO CUT A MITRED CORNER

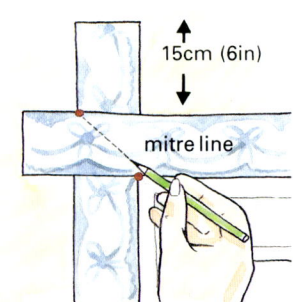  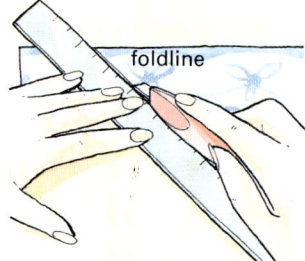 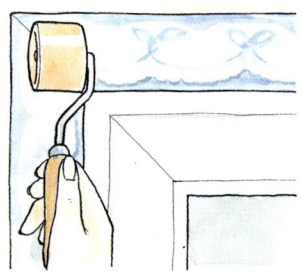

1 Cut and paste the vertical section in place, leaving a 15cm (6in) overlap more than the width of the border. Lay the horizontal strip and mark in pencil on the vertical strip where they intersect at the inner and outer points. Join these lines to make the angle of the mitre. On the vertical section, cut along the line and repaste.

2 Fold along the pencil line of the horizontal strip and place it against the pasted strip to get the right pattern match. When you are satisfied, make a sharp crease at the foldline to match the pencil line.

3 Cut along the foldline on the horizontal section with sharp scissors or a craft knife held against a ruler. Measure up and cut the full length of the horizontal strip, allowing 15cm (6in) overlap at the other end.

4 Paste the horizontal section and butt it up to the other strip. Press firmly in place and wipe surplus adhesive from the wall. Secure the join with a seam roller.

Wallpapering solutions

Even the smallest room can present obstacles to a perfect finish. Though it might seem simple to wallpaper a cloakroom, for example, the small space is likely to have nooks and crannies, recessed windows, a cistern and a small radiator to paper behind. But for each little deviation there is a tried and tested technique.

The most traditional-looking rooms often have complicated interiors. Sloping walls, recessed windows and irregularly shaped rooms present an obvious challenge. Even modern interiors have their own complications, most obviously in the form of fixtures and fittings to do with the conveniences of a contemporary lifestyle. Increasing numbers of electrical appliances in every room mean there is a need for several sockets. Light switches, too, need to be fitted into a wallpapering scheme. Luckily, most of these fitments can be removed – after turning off the electricity – and papered smoothly behind before replacing them.

Even in today's standardized homes doors, windows and recesses come in a variety of shapes and sizes and present their own problems to the decorator. Radiators can be tackled in one of two ways. If they are of the older type of design, or if you feel unsure of how to remove them from the wall bracket, simply paper as far behind them as possible. Alternatively, the newer types can be loosened and swung forward to allow you to paper behind them.

With a little care, all these problem features can be overcome to give a smooth, professional finish to the room.

▼ **Papering a bathroom** Small rooms, with the conveniences of modern life, can be the most difficult to paper because there isn't a lot of space to work in. This Victorian-style bathroom has a towel rail, window sills that jut out on to the adjacent wall and sanitary ware with its associated plumbing – all are tricky shapes needing care to paper around successfully.

SOCKETS AND SWITCHES

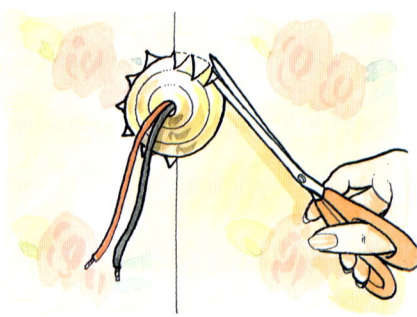

Papering around wall switches If the faceplate is removable, turn off the power at the mains and then unscrew the plate. Make the diagonal cuts but instead of trimming off the flaps, tuck them behind the plate. Do not use this method with foil paper.

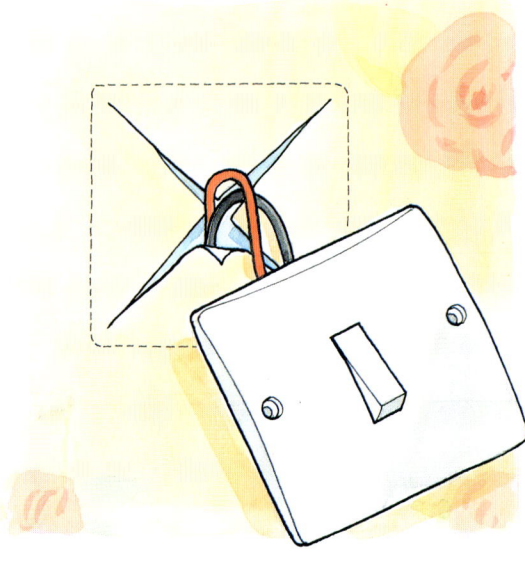

Papering around sockets Turn off power at the mains and remove any light fittings. Paper straight over the the light socket and then use a sharp knife to make diagonal cuts to the corners (or several cuts if it is round). Press the flaps back into position and trim.

DOORS AND WINDOWS

1 Hanging the paper Hang the drop in the normal way, allowing it to hang over the face of the door. Trim paper roughly to the shape of the frame, allowing about 2.5cm (1in) overlap, and make a 12mm (½in) diagonal cut into corner.

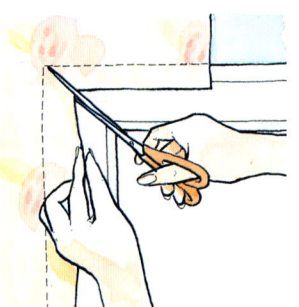

2 Trimming to the corner Brush the paper into the angle between wall and frame, mark a crease line with the back of the scissors and trim.

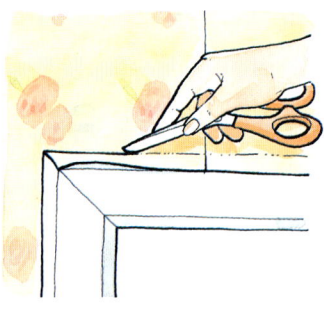

WINDOW RECESS

Where to begin Paper the inside of the recess first, turning a 12mm (½in) flap on to the surrounding wall. Then paper the wall round the window, cutting out the shape exactly.

RADIATORS

Behind a fixed radiator Let the paper hang over the face of the radiator and cut a slit up from the bottom of the length so that the paper can pass either side of the radiator bracket. Across the centre you may find it easier to cut the paper to 20-30cm (8-12in). Tuck the paper behind the radiator and smooth it around the bracket with a long ruler or similar implement to allow you to reach down behind the radiator.

Removing the radiator Hang the paper over the brackets. Make a vertical cut up the bracket and horizontal slits at top and bottom. Smooth the paper each side of the bracket and trim off the excess.

Tongue-and-groove panelling

Lining the walls of a room with wooden panelling adds an old-fashioned warmth and character to more modern country-style decorations. You don't need to clad complete rooms, or even complete walls. If you cut the boards to just below an imaginary picture rail level, tongue and groove panels provide an excellent background for kitchen or alcove shelving or a facing for a redundant chimney breast.

However, panelling the dado or the sides of a bath are the most manageable projects to start on since you will be working with shorter lengths of timber in easily accessible areas. Tongue-and-groove panelling is available in easily assembled kit form for dados from major decorating supply stores; a kit for panelling a dado area generally comes complete with a dado rail and replacement skirting.

The benefits of panelling

Cut short, vertical boards fitted just to dado height and topped with a timber moulding provide a tough, attractive lower surface to the wall area. This is especially advantageous in areas such as halls and stairways which can suffer from rough treatment.

Apart from looking good, panelling has other benefits. It is an excellent way of concealing numerous shortcomings on the surface of the walls, covering old,

▼ **Barely clad**
Teaming simple tongue-and-groove panelling on the side of the bath and the low walls with limed floor boards embodies the spartan approach to a real country feeling.

crumbling or patched plaster and hiding unsightly pipes or cables. Cladding also provides both heat and sound insulation, especially if you place an insulating material like rigid polystyrene or a mineral wool blanket between the battens before you fix the boards in position. Because of the cavity behind the boards, cladding is good at cutting down on condensation, which makes it an excellent wall covering for steamy bathrooms and kitchens.

Choosing materials

In tongue-and-groove boards, one edge of each board has a groove machined along it, while the other has a matching tongue which slots into an adjacent groove when the boards are fixed to the wall. They are available from timber yards and decorating supply superstores.

When estimating quantities of timber required for battens and panelling, sketch a plan of each wall. Take the plan with you to the supplier. Remember each board overlaps along both edges so make allowances for this. Most boards come in 75-100mm (3-4in) widths.

In order to acclimatize the timber to its surroundings and reduce the risk of subsequent warping, store it in the room where you intend to hang it.

Preparing the walls

Cladding can be fixed over any wall surface, so no elaborate preparation is required. But covering the wall with panelling will not cure dampness; it merely hides any sign of damp that may occur, allowing it to spread without your knowledge. It is important, therefore, to solve any possible problems and allow the wall to dry before you start. To stop condensation forming on the inside, you can fix a sheet of polythene to the wall before you fit the battens.

Starting with the battens

The tongue-and-groove boards are usually fixed to the walls by nailing them to a network of timber battens. First decide whether you want to fix the panelling vertically or horizontally; this will determine the alignment of the battens – along the wall for vertical boards, up the wall for horizontal ones.

It is usually simplest to treat shallow skirtings and architraves around doorways and window frames as pre-set battens and fix the boards over them. You can then either leave a gap at the bottom, trim the edges with some beading or fix new mouldings to the panelling. Heavier skirtings and frames which stand proud of the battens must be prised off.

Use lengths of 50 x 25mm (2 x 1in) timber, fixed to the wall at the top and bottom of the planned panelling and at intervals of 400-600mm (16-24in).

On a good wall you should be able to fix the timber to the wall with masonry nails; on crumbling plaster you will need to drill holes and use wall plugs with screws. **Take great care not to drill into cables or pipes buried in the wall, especially around electrical fittings. Check first.**

When fixing battens along the edges of walls, leave about a 12mm (½in) gap. This way you won't have to pin the boards too close to the edge.

Materials

Lengths of 50 x 25mm (2 x 1in) **batten**
Hand drill with no. 8 **wood bit**, no. 12 **masonry bit**, **wallplugs**, no. 8 (2½in) **countersunk wood screws** and **screwdriver**
Tongue-and-groove boards – with special clips in kit form
25mm (1in) **panel pins** or thin **lost head nails** and **hammer**
Chisel and **saw**

FIXING THE BATTENS

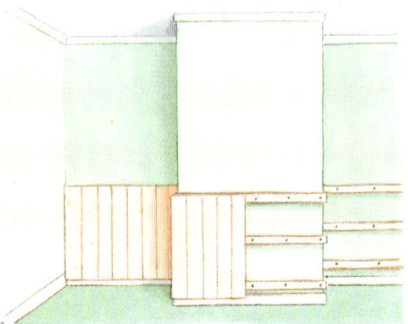

For vertical boards fit rows of horizontal battens to the wall. Drill holes in the battens at 45cm (18in) intervals. Fix the top batten flush with the top of the panelling, the bottom one about 12mm (½in) above the skirting and the middle one between the two. Make sure each batten is straight.

FIXING WITH CLIPS

1 Fixing the first board Use starter clips, if available, to fix the first board in a corner of the room. Pin a clip to each batten close to the corner. Use a spirit level to check that the board will be truly vertical when fixed in position. Trim the tongue from the board and push the cut edge into the starter clips.

FIXING WITH PINS

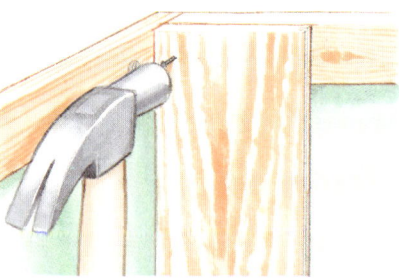

1 Placing the first panel Begin in a corner and place the first panel with the groove towards the corner. Check that the board is vertical with a spirit level, then pin it to each batten, carefully hammering the panel pins through the board about 12mm (½in) in from the groove.

Add extra battens just above skirtings and around door frames and windows to support the edges of the cladding.

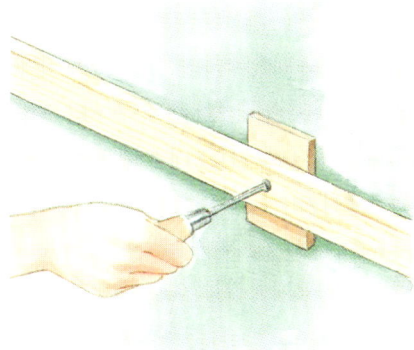

On an uneven surface, cladding is more tricky to install. Hold a length of batten against the wall to check for bumps and hollows. Fix to the highest point and pad out behind the battens where dips occur with scraps of plywood. Check the face is even with a spirit level.

Around sockets and switches cut short lengths of batten to butt up as closely as possible to the fitting and use panel adhesive to fix them.

2 Using standard clips Fit standard clips into the groove in the board at each batten position and pin to the batten to secure. Slot the tongue of the next board into the groove.

3 Fitting firmly Knock home securely with a hammer using a spare piece of board as a tamping block. Then fix the clips as before and continue fitting the remaining boards in the same way until you come to the final board in the run.

Truly straight
Always make sure the first board is precisely vertical or horizontal with the aid of a spirit level before securing in place, rather than following the edge of a wall which might well be out of true. Any gap in the corner can be covered with beading.

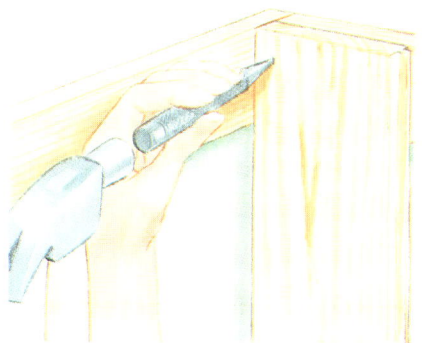

2 Hiding the pins Use a nail punch to drive each head just below the surface. If pin positions show when the panelling is finished fill holes with wood filler.

3 Angling the pins Fix a second pin through the board into each batten. Position it at the point where the tongue meets the board and angle it at 45° into the full-width board so that the tongue is left free for the next board to slot over it.

4 Fixing subsequent lengths Push the next board in so that the tongue on the first board is hidden in the new groove. Fix this second board with one pin in each batten as in step 3.

5 Fitting the final board The last board on any wall will have to be face nailed like the first.

FITTING ROUND CORNERS

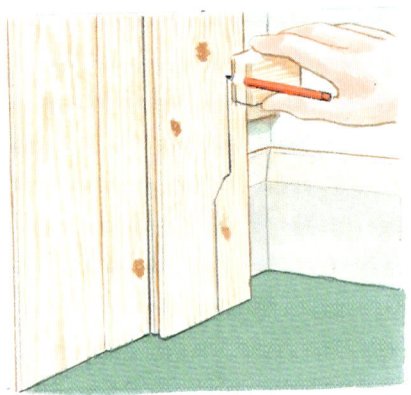

Fitting internal corners When you reach the first corner, scribe and cut the last board to fit the space left as tightly as possible. Then butt the first board on the adjacent wall up to cover the cut edge.

Fitting external corners Where possible, work away from an external corner. Fix the boards with grooves towards the corner and so that they just touch, then fill the angled space with beading.

FIT AROUND OBSTACLES

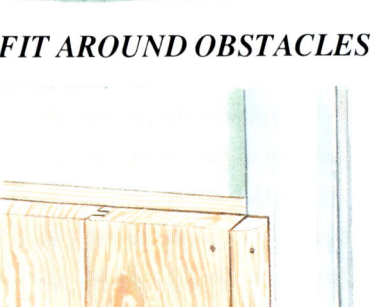

Fitting around doors Secure the last board to the batten adjacent to the architrave. Then fill the board and architrave junction with beading.

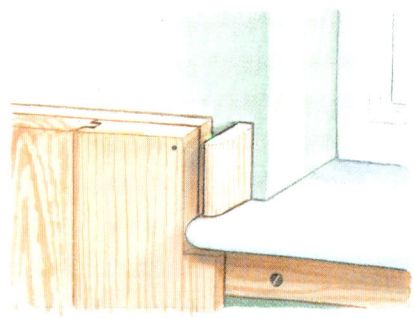

Fitting around windows Finish the panelling just short of the reveal and cover the batten and board edges with beading. If you want to take the panelling into the reveal, then stick a board, cut to fit, to the reveal wall. Finish in the same way as an external corner.

Fitting over sockets and switches
Cut the boards so that the switch and socket plate will just cover the cut edges. Pin the boards to the glued battens around the socket or switch.

Before dealing with sockets and light switches, be sure **to turn off the power at the mains box**. Then loosen off the switch or socket faceplate and check there is enough slack in the circuit cables to pull the unit forward to the boards. If you don't fully understand electric circuits, it is probably wise to call in an electrician to advise you.

Finishing the panelling
Tidying up the corners However carefully you work, the cut edges of the boards in the corners always look a little uneven. Neaten them off by adding a length of quadrant or scotia beading.
Replacing or re-newing skirting boards Although the tongue-and-groove boards can be left plain, pin a strip of new skirting board at the base of the panelling for a trim finish.
Trimming with a dado rail A wooden moulding adds a perfect finish to the top of the dado panelling. Pin and glue with pva glue into position, or use special clips provided in some kits. Either spread a neatening skim of plaster filler along the shallow ledge of batten, board and dado rail, or fix a length of beading along the top of the dado rail to fill the gap between the wall and the wood and give it a neat finish.

▲ **Colourful gutters**
A faint shadow of blue-grey stain accenting the between-board channels looks effective when repeated on the brackets and shelves.

Finishing the timber
Apply a finish to the panelling as soon as possible to prevent damage or marking and avoid boards absorbing moisture.

The timber can be stained darker, to mimic more valuable hardwood, or left natural and polished or varnished. Alternatively, take advantage of the new pastel and bright colour wood finishes that add paint colour but still allow the grain of the wood to show through.

For a subtle effect, consider painting a row of boards in gradually deepening tones of one colour or using a range of pastels to form stripes in pale shades.

Wooden floors

Choosing the right floor surface or floor covering for the rooms in your home is important as it can often be a major investment. The flooring should take into account the kind of activities which take place in a room, as well as complement the style of furnishing and the colour scheme. Above all, most floors need to be practical surfaces.

An entrance hall which gets a lot of wear needs a hardwearing surface in a colour which will not show the dirt; a kitchen floor which is liable to be splashed with grease needs a surface which can be cleaned easily. A bathroom needs a surface which resists water, while a bedroom floor should be soft underfoot and does not need to be as hardwearing as the floor covering in a room used by all the family.

Country style floors

When considering flooring with a country look, natural materials immediately come to mind. Traditionally, polished wood has been used, with rush matting and rugs to soften the hard surfaces and add warmth and colour. Styles and building methods change and new materials are used in construction, so today's

▲ **A polished surface**
Rich dark wood which has been cared for and polished over the years has a wonderful warm glow. The furniture in the room has been chosen to match the floor – a rag rug at the side of the bed would be a welcome addition.

modern homes do not often have hardwood floorboards. If your house does not have the kind of flooring you ideally want there are ways of changing the existing floor using modern equivalents which are relatively easy to lay.

▲ A varnished finish
This modern woodstrip floor has been finished with a coloured satin varnish to protect the surface and make it easy to clean and maintain. Once varnished, the surface will withstand a reasonable amount of wear and tear and retain its shine with an occasional polish.

◀ Herringbone style
Woodstrip flooring can be laid in decorative patterns such as this popular herringbone design which is quite easy to do. In this hallway the pattern is laid down the centre, with a straight strip edging.

The warmth of wood

Old polished wooden floorboards which have been cared for develop a rich shine but few of us are lucky enough to live in a house with such natural beauty. In some older houses, if you take up the carpet, you may find that the floorboards are in a good enough condition to consider sanding and polishing them and then leaving them uncovered. Hiring a sander to smooth the surface and remove any paint or stain is a possibility but before you start take a really good look at the floor to see if it really is worth all the effort. If one or two boards are very worn but the rest of the floor is in a good condition, consider taking them up and re-laying them the other way up rather than replacing them altogether. Remember to punch in all the nails before you start sanding.

If the floor is very uneven you could consider laying one of the wood strip floorings available from do-it-yourself stores. You will need to prepare the surface by laying down sheets of hardboard first.

In modern houses the floors are likely to be made of concrete on the ground floor and chipboard sheets on the upper floors. If floorboards are used they are probably made from pine and of a quality which is not suitable for staining or polishing. If you wish to lay a wood floor then modern wood strips or wood mosaic floor tiles are easily laid over these surfaces.

▲ **Bleached out**
While most varnishes and stains darken the original colour of the wood, bleaching can do the opposite. These floorboards have been lightened to match the furniture and sealed for protection.

◀ **A lighter touch**
These old floorboards have been sanded and varnished, keeping the original light oak colour. To have stained them to match the door and skirting board would make the hallway very dark. A bright rug adds a welcoming touch.

Where to use them

Wood floors are commonly found in sitting rooms, dining rooms or hallways and although there is nothing to prevent you having them elsewhere in the house you should consider the following points before making a decision.

Unless they are really well sealed, wood floors are best avoided in bathrooms and kitchens as the wood will absorb water and spills.

A wooden floor in a bedroom could be a little cold to walk on in bare feet so you will need to have a cosy bedside rug to avoid getting out of bed on to a bare floor in the morning.

Walking about on a wooden floor can be noisy, particularly for anyone in the room below, so they are not ideal for use in upstairs rooms or in flats. If you are considering a wooden floor upstairs, consider taking up the floorboards to add some sound insulation underneath.

Types of wooden flooring

Woodstrip flooring is available in two main types – solid planks or laminated strips with a decorative surface veneer. The length of the strips can vary from as little as 40cm (16in) to 180cm (70in) and widths range from 7cm (2 $^3/_4$in) up to 20cm (8in). Both types are usually made up from strips of wood which are shorter and narrower than the finished panel and the veneered type may resemble one continuous plank or have a basketweave effect.

Both types are generally tongued and grooved on both long and short edges for easy fitting but some are designed to be fixed to a timber sub-floor by secret nailing while others can be loose-laid using ingenious metal clips to hold them together. If you are likely to need access to underfloor services such as wiring or piping choose the type which is not nailed to the floor.

Another alternative is wood mosaic floor tiles. These are square tiles made up from a number of small fingers of wood. The fingers themselves may be solid hardwood or veneer on a cheaper soft-wood backing and are usually laid in a basketweave pattern, although other arrangements are also available.

Laminated veneers are generally pre-finished while solid strips may be finished or need sealing once they have been laid.

Types of wood

A wide range is available including elm, oak, ash, beech and maple. When choosing the kind of wood bear in mind the colour scheme of the room. Some woods have a warm reddish tone, others are very pale with an almost pastel look. If there will be any wooden furniture in the room choose a floor to match.

The following chapter describes how to lay modern woodstrip flooring. There's guidance on sanding floorboards on pages 41–44; pages 45–48 present ways of decorating a wooden floor.

▲**Subtle variations of colour**
Parquet flooring combines strips of wood, often in different shades, which are made up into tiles. Traditionally the strips are set at right angles to each other to create a basketweave effect. The tiles are usually made up in groups of four or sixteen, ready to be laid.

Laying a woodstrip floor

Wooden floors are among the most naturally attractive forms of flooring. Unfortunately, if you long for rooms with 'bare board' floors, you may be disappointed when you lift your carpet and discover what defects it has kept hidden. Sadly, not all old floorboards are worth the effort of sanding and polishing, particularly if they are littered with unsightly nail heads and have large draughty gaps between them. And if the sub-floor is concrete, laying a wooden floor on top would appear to be an extremely costly job best left to the professionals.

To meet the growing trend towards natural finishes in the home, however, there is a perfectly practical solution – long narrow strips of wood, about 1cm (3/8in) thick, in kit form which are easy to lay on any sub-floor. Whilst woodstrip is certainly not cheap to put down in the first place, it is very durable. Many manufacturers claim a life of at least 10 years for the original finish, after which the surface can be sanded down and resealed.

Made from solid wood or with a beech, pine or oak veneer on a particle board core, the strips are tongued-and-grooved on their edges so they simply slot together. They can be secured by nailing to a wooden sub-floor, fixed with clips set in a groove on the underside of the boards or glued firmly with PVA or wood glue where the floor is concrete. Consult the manufacturer's instructions for the particular boards you buy.

Measuring up

Wood strips are sold in a variety of lengths and widths – 200 x 20cm (78¾ x 7⅞in) is the average size, which is enough to cover 3.2 sq m (3½ sq yd). Most manufacturers of kits give guides on average coverage per pack of boards together with recommendations about suitable sub-floors on the packaging.

▲ **All the comforts of wood**
Knotty woodstrip flooring enhances the rustic charm of a cottage living-room. The floor feels warm and comfortable to walk on; a gay rug simply breaks up the expanse of bare boards for a cosier look.

Work out how much you need by measuring the dimensions of the room and drawing an accurate plan on a piece of graph paper to calculate the total floor area. Add an extra five per cent for cutting and wastage.

You can also use your plan to work out the best method for laying the flooring; strip flooring must be laid across existing floorboards or parallel to a light source coming through the window. Pay special attention to planning doorways, alcoves and bays, trying to fit in whole boards where unsightly cutting would show.

Good groundwork
Check the condition of the sub-floor.
On wooden floorboards If the existing floorboards are sound, you may only need to hammer home projecting nail heads and sand smooth any raised areas; if it is poor, the floor should be first covered with a layer of 3mm (⅛in) plywood to create a smooth level surface. PVC or linoleum floor coverings can remain in place.
On a concrete sub-floor you must be perfectly sure there's no suggestion of damp; check it out by taping a piece of glass to the floor for several days. If moisture collects on the underside, you have a problem which may need specialist attention. Any irregularities should be filled and the floor surface thoroughly cleaned. Then give it a continuous waterproof coating either with a polyurethane sealing compound or sheets of 0.2mm (0.008in) thick plastic foil.

Before you lay strip flooring on any surface, it makes sense to place a layer of insulating material in between.

Points to watch
Doors Remember that the new flooring will raise the original floor level significantly. If this is likely to impede the opening and closing of any doors, you will have to take them off their hinges before you lay the new floor – otherwise you could be trapped in the room behind an unopenable door! Before re-hanging the door, plane or saw off the bottom edge.
Matching edges Work out how many boards are needed across the room. If the last board is less than 5cm (2in) wide, then cut the first to an equal width so they match up at either side.
Expansion gap Wood expands and contracts, almost imperceptibly, with changes in temperature and humidity. It will eventually warp unless you allow an expansion gap all around the edges of the room. About 1cm (⅜in) is adequate and you can conceal it with the existing skirting boards, if you are prepared to remove them before starting work. You will have to lever them off carefully against a wooden block to minimize any damage to the wall.

Alternatively you can fill the gap with quadrant or scotia beading pinned to the skirting itself. It will be simpler if, before fixing, you paint the beading to match the skirting boards or stain it to match the floor. Then touch up or fill the pin heads once the beading is secured in place.
Acclimatization Allow wood strips to acclimatize in the room in which they will be laid. Store in unopened packages at room temperature for at least 48 hours before laying.

Materials
Hammer, chisel and a **small crowbar**
Fine-toothed saw and **fretsaw**
A **tamping block** made from a piece of softwood
Spacer blocks of wood about 1cm (⅜in) thick
Pencil, ruler and **adjustable template**
PVA or **wood glue**, **clips** or **nails**, depending on the fixing method

---

LAYING WOODSTRIP FLOORING

1 Laying the first board Place the first board with the grooved edge to the wall. Place spacer blocks, cut to the size of the expansion gap required, between the board and the wall.

2 Laying the second board Lay further boards, end to end, to complete the first row. Fit them dry first and trim the end plank so that it falls 1cm (⅜in) from the wall. To do this, place the last board so that tongue lies next to tongue, with the end butted to the wall and a spacer block in position. Mark where to saw and cut to length.

3a If using secret nailing, drive the fixing pins at an angle of 45° down through the tongues into the wooden sub-floor, punching the heads into the angle but taking care not to over drive them or the tongue will split. Nails should be spaced about 30cm (12in) apart. Punch heads below the surface; they will be covered by the next strip of board.

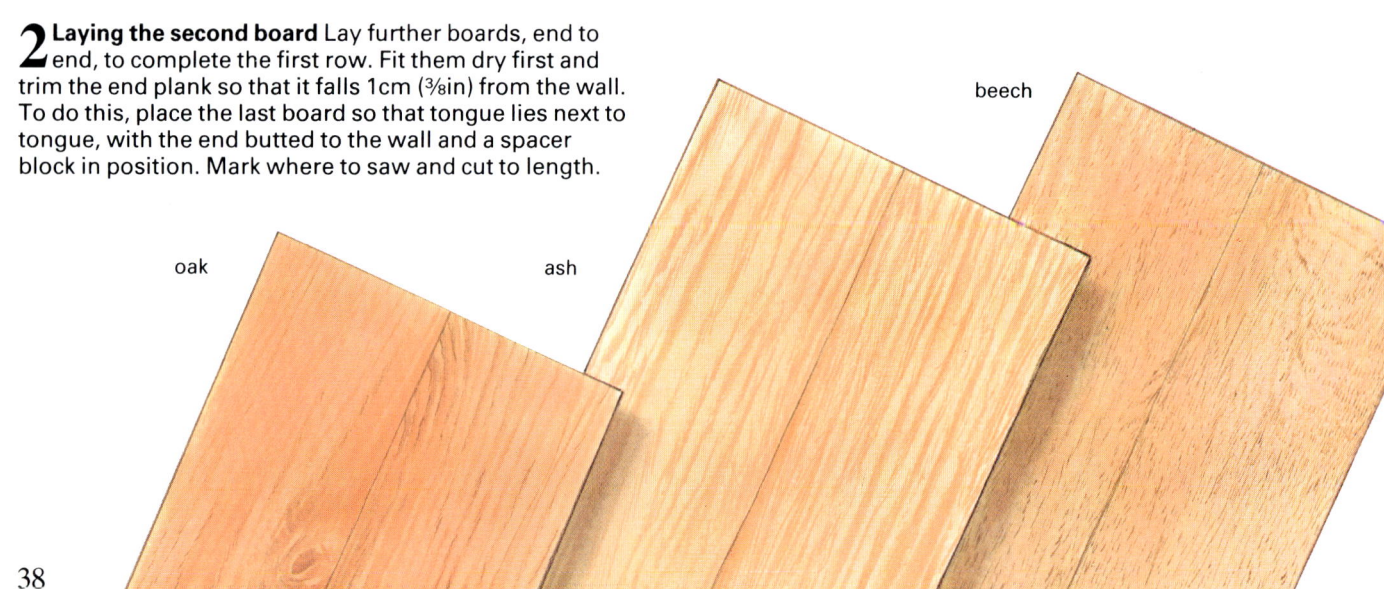

oak   ash   beech

3b If using fixing clips, the method of fixing depends on the system. The type shown here, you just tap the clips into the grooves in the underside of the boards, at the recommended intervals, and lay them against the spacer blocks. When you come to fix subsequent boards make sure you stagger the positions of the fixing clips.

3c If gluing the ends as they butt together, most systems recommend PVA adhesive. Apply a little adhesive to each plank and tap into position, wiping away any surplus adhesive with a damp cloth. Use a string line to check the boards are straight; if they need adjusting, remove, or add, spacer blocks accordingly.

4 Fitting the next row Lay subsequent rows, with the joints staggered – they should not be closer than 30cm (12in) – by offering their grooved edges up to the tongued edges. Start the second row with the piece of board left over from the first. Tap into place with hammer and tamping block and secure as before.

5 Fixing the last strip When you get to the last row, measure the plank of woodstrip to fill the remaining gap by placing one board on top of the previous one and another with the tongue butting against the wall.

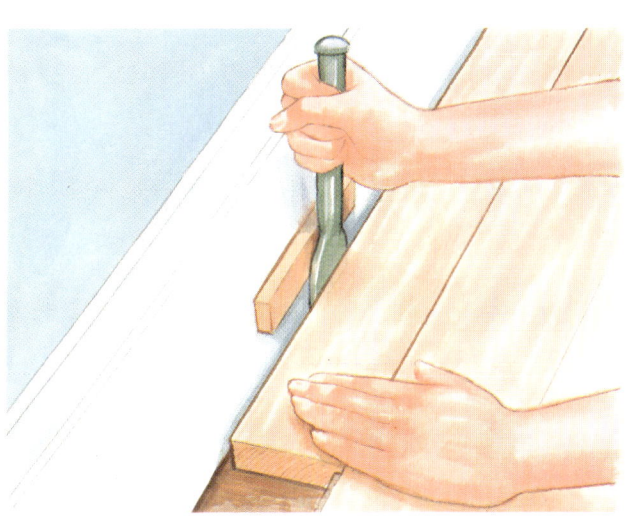

6 Easing into place Rule in pencil along the cutting line, saw to size and then ease into place using the bolster and hammer to press the boards home tight.

7 Replacing the skirting board Remove spacer blocks, replace skirting or fit beading strip to cover the gap.

FITTING AROUND AWKWARD SHAPES

Measure and mark the position of the pipe on the board. Saw two parallel cuts in from the edge for the required distance using a fretsaw, carefully sawing in a circle at the inner end to fit around the pipe. Slide in place up to the pipe. Trim to fit if necessary, leaving a 1cm (⅜in) gap between the edge and the wall.

Where planks meet awkward obstacles like door frames, use an adjustable metal template with movable rods or a paper pattern to transfer the outline of the obstacle to the board, ready for cutting. You may need a fine fretsaw to make all the intricate cut-outs necessary for a precise fit.

Finishing at a doorway Lay the appropriate threshold strip to provide a neat ramp from one room to the next.

> ### *tip*
>
> **Caring for wood floors**
> **Keep clean** Sweep or vacuum regularly and clean with a mild cleaning agent and damp cloth. Never use abrasive materials.
> **Keep dry** Avoid over-wetting. Wooden floors are unsuitable for shower areas and utility rooms.
> **Protection** Stop dirt at the entrance with a door mat and deal with accidental spillages and stains immediately they occur. Take care when moving furniture; always lift rather than drag it across the floor.

◀ *Wood sense*
Natural wood proves to be a practical and good-looking choice of flooring in the kitchen. For a start, woodstrip is easy to clean, which makes it very hygienic. At the same time the hardwearing finish is robust enough to stand up to non-stop household traffic. But notice how the wooden flooring is not carried through into the utility room next door where it would not benefit from a regular soaking. When the floor is teamed up with matching beech units and worktops, it creates a smart working area.

Sanding a wooden floor

The natural good looks of bare floorboards fit perfectly into a country design scheme. Their rugged simplicity can either be used to set off a slightly rustic type of decoration or provide a moderating, plainer contrast to a more flamboyant style.

Most homes are fitted with pine floorboards but a few lucky houses have oak boards. Although plain wooden boards provide hardwearing and attractive flooring, in time they inevitably become dirty and dented and then get covered with carpet or lino tiles. Lifting an existing floor covering may well reveal that the floorboards underneath are unfit for immediate display. However, a thorough sanding will remove the old surface and expose fresh, clean wood, which can then be protected by a sealer to give an inexpensive, durable and very beautiful floor.

Hiring the equipment

Preparing the floor involves sanding the floorboards, first with a powered drum sander and then with a small edging sander, which gets into areas the larger one cannot reach. You can hire these from your local tool rental centre.

Ask for a demonstration of the machines so that you know how to operate them and be sure to take plenty of abrasive sheets and belts of all grades away with you. Also buy or hire a face mask and safety goggles at the same time, so that you aren't choked or blinded by the fine sawdust. Change the

▲ **Baring the boards**
Brilliant sunshine streaming through the window throws a spotlight across bare floorboards and highlights the natural beauty of well-waxed wood.

filter in your face mask regularly to prevent it getting clogged. Ear protectors to muffle the noise are also a good idea, although not essential.

Ensure that the sander picks up as much dust as possible by emptying the collecting bag frequently into heavy duty plastic rubbish bags; collecting bags have been known to catch fire spontaneously when overfull. Never throw the dust on a fire later; the fine particles can flash into fierce flames.

Preparing the floorboards

Lift the existing floor covering and inspect the boards underneath. Check for sagging boards, which are a sign of damaged joists; lever the floorboard up to examine the joists beneath. Rotten timber and boards may have to be treated or replaced professionally. Also look out for any tell-tale signs of woodworm which you can treat with an insecticide.

Using a claw hammer, remove the tacks or nails that were used to hold the old floor covering in place and watch out for protruding floorboard nail heads as well. Knock these back into the boards using a hammer and nail punch. If the abrasive sheet on a sanding machine catches on a nail during use, it can rip with a shocking bang.

Regular wide gaps between the floorboards become dust traps and an annoying source of cold draughts. They are most easily remedied by lifting the boards and re-laying them. The occasional unsightly split between two boards can be filled with strips of wood or papier-mâché. Creaking floorboards are often loose; knocking in extra flooring nails will stop any movement.

Materials
Overalls or old clothes
Face mask with spare filters
Goggles and **ear defenders**
Masking tape
Claw hammer, **nail punch** and **floor nails**
Drum and **small belt edging sander**
Coarse, **medium** and **fine abrasive strips**
Vacuum cleaner, **white spirit** and **rags**
Sealant and **brushes**.

A range of strips

Sealant

Face mask and ear defenders

Gloves

Goggles

SANDING A WOOD FLOOR

1 Cleaning the floor Preliminary cleaning exposes the true condition of the boards before you start sanding. Vacuum away any dirt and, if necessary, scrub the floor using the minimum of hot, soapy water. Wetting the floor will raise the grain which will need sanding off when it is dry. Where there is a heavy build up of wax, remove some of it by rubbing with wire wool soaked in white spirit.

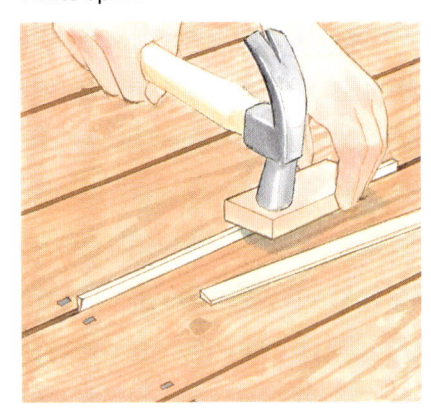

2 Blocking the big gaps Plug any odd large gaps between the floor boards with thin strips of timber tapered into a slight wedge. Spread both sides with glue before knocking them down between the boards with a hammer. Use a wooden block to protect the floorboards. Then plane them level with the floor.

3 Filling the narrow gaps Mix some torn up newspaper, wallpaper paste and boiling water together in a bowl and add some wood stain to match the colour of the boards. Stuff this papier-mâché into the small gaps between the boards with a filling knife. Leave the filler slightly proud of the surface because it might shrink as it dries. Sand it smooth when hard.

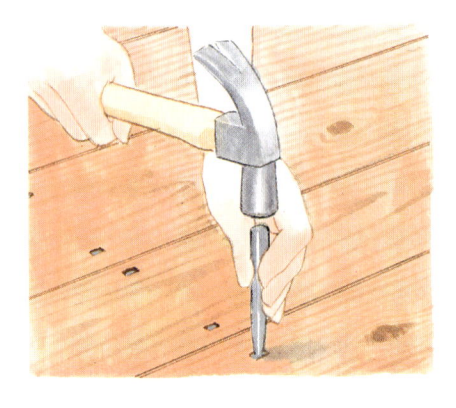

4 Knocking in raised nails Go over the floor very carefully, punching down any protruding nail heads with a hammer and a nail punch. Fill any small hollows with wood filler later. Fix any loose boards with extra nails tapped in near the old ones to avoid pipes and electric cables.

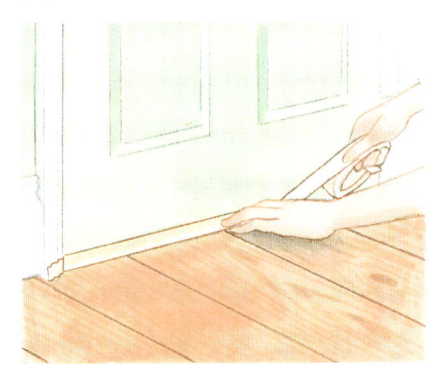

5 Sealing the room The fine dust from sanding penetrates everywhere so clear the room completely of furnishings. Then, when you are ready to start sanding, and have all the equipment you need in the room close the door to the rest of the house. Seal around the frame with masking tape and open the windows for ventilation.

6 Starting the sander Fit a coarse abrasive sheet, making sure it is taut and firmly locked in place. Never start the machine while the drum is resting on the ground. Tilt the machine backwards, switch on and lower it gradually to the floor as it builds up speed. Be prepared to be tugged forwards as the drum contacts the floor.

▼ In the wood
With their pronounced grain and warm honey colour, stripped pine floorboards supply the perfect complement to the light and airy atmosphere in this garden room. Sealed with a coat of varnish, they are able to withstand any hard wear from dirty shoes traipsing through.

7 Beginning to sand Start by working diagonally back and forth across the room at 45° to the boards. Avoid stopping while the machine is running as you risk gouging the boards; tip it back as you turn at the end of each run instead, avoiding the skirtings. Check the abrasive sheet occasionally to make sure it is not clogged; change to a fresh piece when it becomes worn. Continue with the coarse abrasive sheets until the worst of the marks have gone.

8 Honing the finish Change to a medium abrasive strip and go on working diagonally across the floor. Next, sand the floor parallel to the floorboards, again going over each strip in both directions, minding the skirtings as you turn. Then switch to fine abrasive and repeat the whole process again. It's also a good idea to vacuum the floor from time to time to minimize the amount of fine dust flying around.

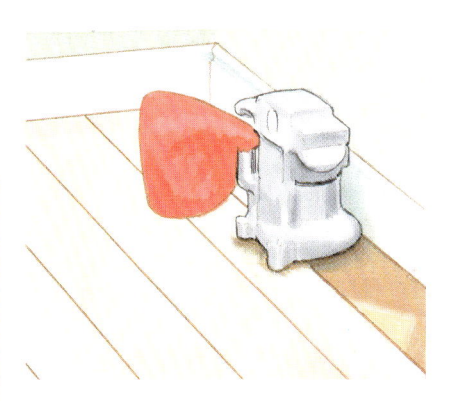

9 Going round the edges Now switch to the smaller edging sander to tackle the borders of the room. Work with coarse and medium abrasive sheets to clear the marks and fine ones for a smooth finish.

10 Cleaning up the dust After sanding, vacuum the floor thoroughly, along with the skirtings, door and window frames and mop up the last specks of dust with a dampened cloth. Leave for 24 hours to let the dust settle before vacuuming again. Finally, give the boards a wipe with white spirit to remove all dust before sealing.

---

tip

Safe sanding
Don't let children anywhere near the sanding machine; always unplug the machine when changing the sanding strips; keep the sander's flex out of harm's way during use by draping it over your shoulder.

Sealing the floor

Once the bare wood of the boards has been exposed it needs to be protected from staining and damage with some form of durable sealer.

Polyurethane varnish is the usual choice of sealer. It is easy to apply, using at least three, and preferably four, coats of cover. Thin the first coat of varnish with white spirit, following the maker's instructions, to encourage the sealant to permeate into the wood. Apply the varnish with a 100mm (4in) brush, working along the grain. After each coat is dry, sand the surface lightly using fine glasspaper on a block or a wad of medium grade steel wool. Vacuum again and wipe over with the white-spirit-soaked cloth before applying the next coat of varnish.

Solvent-free varnishes are more user and environmentally friendly. They combine all the traditional benefits of a tough, scratch-resistant surface with a low level of odour and a rapid drying time. Each coat is 'touch' dry in only 20 minutes and you can apply another coat after two hours. Best of all, when you have finished the job, you can simply wash out your brushes in water.

Stain and varnish stain The natural tones of the wood can be altered by staining, or by using a coloured polyurethane varnish. Stain on its own is applied before sealing: use a spirit-based stain, and apply it with a cloth pad, not a brush. This gives a more even coverage over the wooden boards.

When using varnish stain, apply a thinned coat of clear varnish first. This lightly seals the surface so that it will absorb the colour evenly. Follow that with two or more coloured coats. Finish with another clear coat of gloss, matt or silk, according to your choice.

▲ **A warm footing**
Lovely old floorboards are the ideal surface to enhance the country mood of a cottage-style bedroom.

▼ **Immaculate planking**
Expanses of brand new boards provide a fresh, easy-to-clean floor that suits open layouts.

Decorated wooden floors

Once you decide to opt for a wooden floor, rather than for tiles, vinyl flooring or carpet, you have many options on how to treat it. Those lucky enough to have a house with very high quality floorboards, mellowed with age to a rich attractive shade, will probably neither want nor need to do anything to enhance the beauty of the wood. Simple varnishing or waxing will be enough.

If, however, your floorboards leave something to be desired, you have a good choice of decorative finishes: dyeing, staining, painting, and stencilling being the most popular. You can treat large areas like the hall, stairs and landings, living rooms, kitchens and bathrooms in this way. If you prepare the wood properly and apply several coats of varnish over your work, the finish will last for ages, and the mellowing effect of time and sunlight will make your efforts prettier as the years go by.

Decorating your wooden floor is an infinitely cheaper option than carpeting, but it is very time consuming, and the floor you are working on will be out of commission for a couple of weeks while you first prepare it, then paint it, then finally treat it with several coats of varnish. It is really important that all decorative finishes are applied on clean, bare wood, sanded, filled where necessary, scrubbed and rubbed with white spirit.

▲ **A stencilled rug**
A stencilled border with a circular central motif gives the effect of a carpet on this wooden kitchen floor. Only three colours have been used in the design but each colour has been shaded from dark to light to vary the intensity.

Base coats
Lightening and bleaching At this stage you may decide that the basic colour of your floorboards is too dark, or has yellowed over the years. To lighten it apply a lavish coat of white, oil-based paint. Wait a few minutes, then rub the paint off with a rag. White residues will remain in the cracks and pores. This forms a good base for colourless varnish. Alternatively you can bleach the floor by scrubbing it with household bleach and then rinsing off with clean water, but varnishing over bleach you may still end up with a yellowish cast, so lightening with paint may be a better option for a really pale floor.

Dyeing and staining When you dye or stain floorboards you will still be able to see the grain and notches in the wood as these finishes are transparent. Take the natural warm colour of most woods into account when choosing a colour. When using dyes and stains, build up the colour gradually to get the effect you want.

Dyeing You can use ordinary fabric, leather or carpet dyes, but make up the solution with half the specified amount of water and apply two or three coats, according to how intense a colour you want, before varnishing.

Staining With the staining process the colour goes deeper into the wood. There is a good range of traditional wood colours to choose from, from palest ash blond to the colour of darkest oak. You can also buy bright stains in reds, blues and greens. There are various different kinds of wood stains on the market, but for floors, you will find that an oil-based stain produces the best and most even finish.

Staining suggestions Untreated floorboards tend to be very pale, and you can keep this look by simply sealing them. However, if you want to make them look warmer and more distinguished you can stain them in the light honey shade that we associate with polished pine, or a deeper, richer, reddy-orange colour for a much warmer look. If you plan to stencil or paint designs on to your floor, you will still probably want to stain the boards first.

Both dyes and stains can be used to create a lively effect in which each individual floorboard is stained in a different shade. Try a combination of reds, oranges and light browns for a warm feel; use blues, greens and chalky whites for a cool effect.

Staining works very well with stencils; try a design in various woody shades such as chestnut, spicy brown and mahogany on light, honey-stained floorboards to create a marvellous marquetry effect that will mellow beautifully.

Painting With floorboards that do not bear close inspection, a coat or two of paint on a prepared surface will work wonders.

A floor painted in a single colour can provide the perfect background for several brightly coloured rugs or a larger carpet. Make sure the colour tones with the rugs you plan to use or the furnishings in the room.

Using the same technique as for staining, paint each board in a different colour. A child's bedroom or playroom would look very jolly and be very hardwearing with floorboards painted in bright primary colours and sealed with multiple layers of varnish.

For the more ambitious, the possibilities with paint are endless. Once you have applied your basic colour (two coats of flat, oil-based paint is best, as you can make the final effect as glossy as you like with varnish) you can give your imagination free rein. Many floor paint effects imitate other floor coverings – one simple but very dramatic effect is to paint a chequer board arranged in a diamond pattern to look like tiles. Traditionally this is done in black and white, but if your floor area is small, it could look better in subtler shades, in soft grey and white, for instance, or sepia and ivory.

▲ **Painted to match**
If your floorboards are not good enough quality to paint or stain you could lay sheets of hardboard, nailing them to the boards, and then prime and paint the surface. A stencil was made from the boldly patterned fabric for use on the floor.

▲ **A hint of a colour**
The blue theme has been carried through on to the floor of this pretty bedroom. The floorboards have been sanded and then stained a pale bluish-grey to match the painted and stained furniture. The wood takes up the stain unevenly which gives a textured feel to the surface.

◀ **A stained pattern**
This simple diamond pattern is achieved by drawing a squared grid pattern on the floor and then using masking tape to outline the areas of the floor to be stained. A geometric pattern like this looks effective used in a hall or lobby.

Stencilling Using stencils, you can create painted rugs or carpets, repeating the same design again and again, and surrounding the whole with a stencilled border. This looks especially good on a floor stained in a light colour, with the stencilled motifs in shades of dark red, brown and russet, or in transparent jewel-like reds, blues and greens. On a bedroom floor, a really pale wood base could be stencilled in transparent pastel shades.

To keep your stencilling simple, you can stick to just doing a decorative border around the walls, leaving the centre of the floor free for a rug or carpet; alternatively you could just do one large stencil in the centre, and leave the rest of the floor plain. If you live in a self-contained house and can cope with the noise, a decorated wooden staircase can be immensely attractive; leave the treads plain, but stencil motifs on to the risers, or simply stencil borders all the way up on both sides of the stairs.

Polishing off

Varnish The hardest wearing finish for a wooden floor is polyurethane varnish, which is heat and stain resistant, easy to apply and easy to clean afterwards. It comes in matt, semi-gloss or gloss finishes, and you can get it in a clear or a tinted finish. When you apply it the floor must be clean and dust free and you must wait for each coat to dry completely before you apply the next. You will need at least three coats in a room with light wear, and at least five in a hall or kitchen or living room. Renew the varnish every couple of years.

Sealing Floor seal is easy to apply, as you can simply swab it on with cloth, working first across the grain, and then with the grain for subsequent coats. Sand the floor lightly between coats. Like varnish, you should re-apply it when it wears thin, first removing all dirt and grease with a sugar soap solution.

Waxing There is nothing quite like the shine and wonderful smell of a floor that has been polished with beeswax, but achieving this finish requires hard work and lots of elbow grease, starting with making the polish. Modern wax polishes are easier to apply and tougher wearing, but waxing is still not an easy option.

You must first seal the floor with a coat of floor seal, allow it to dry and then sand it down. Then apply the beeswax polish or modern commercial wax polish with a soft brush. Leave it to dry, and shine it with first a soft shoe brush, and then a soft cloth.

▲ **Beautiful borders**
A simple border stencil worked in two colours around the edge of a room. Mark the stencil positions carefully so that the effect is visually satisfying. Here the motif is centred

◄ **Zigzag effects**
The strip floor laid in a herringbone pattern has been stained in three different colours, the colour changing with each board. Use masking tape and stain all the boards in one colour before moving on to the next.

Staining wood

Staining timber is a way of changing the wood's colour without sacrificing the character of the grain and knots. This can be done discreetly using wood tones to improve the natural shade or imitate a more expensive timber. Or you can completely transform the appearance of the wood with a whole spectrum of un-wood-like rainbow colours. Brilliant patterns and motifs can be developed from a widely varied palette of colours to pick out moulded details in carved wood and cheer up timber.

In contrast, modern pastel, semi-translucent, grain-displaying paints mimic the soft, faded appeal and weathered finish of old country cottage joinery and furniture. By reproducing the muted colours and distressed finish of genuinely matured rustic features, they can blend new timber articles with old or bring recently stripped older pieces back to life. The effect works equally well on floorboards and panelling, giving the timber an instantly seasoned quality and the room a peaceful atmosphere.

▲ **In the pink**
The warm tones of a pastel pink paint stain successfully soften and meld bare floorboards into a comfortable bedroom decor. The same stain is used again on the bedhead and skirting boards to complete the picture.

Objects for staining

Wooden furniture responds well to staining, either to restore its original hue or mellow new pieces to blend in with older ones. Old pine pieces that have been stripped can often look slightly grey and bleached; a coat or two of a golden stain re-develops its former warmth.

For pine, avoid red tones of stain, like mahogany, which are better for close-grained woods. Antique pine tones are available, but test them first. If necessary, mix different tones until you achieve the desired effect.

Skirtings and doors Staining rather than painting woodwork around the house makes a pleasant change, presenting a more natural or delicate look than conventional gloss and eggshell finishes. Slightly subdued, worn shades integrate beautifully with muted pastels and sheer fabrics, creating a soft focus in the room.

Timber floorboards or panelling offer a broad surface for colour treatment. Decorating a wooden floor is infinitely cheaper than laying carpet or tiles. Already divided into parallel strips, the boards can be stained in stripes, panels, zigzags or mosaics of different shades.

Staining a chequerboard layout simulates the crisp, clean lines of a tiled floor very realistically. Mark out the grid carefully on the floor before you start working in the stains, using masking tape to define the margins. As an extra precaution to prevent the stain bleeding from one area to another, score the borders of the pattern elements lightly with a sharp knife.

Household equipment Plain wooden items around the house gain individuality when stained, particularly if you add a special pattern or motif of your own for extra distinction. In the kitchen a bread bin or paper roll dispenser can be picked out in a rustic stain. In the bathroom, towel rails and accessories retain a naturally grained appearance while adopting a colour that ties in with the rest of the design scheme.

Types of stain

Stains for wood fall into two main types: those, usually put on with a cloth, that sink into the wood but give no surface protection, and those which are incorporated in a varnish so that colour and protection are imparted at the same time (see page 56).

Stain on its own comes in a range of wood and primary colours. They can be water or oil-based. Many stains tend to soak in quickly which can make it difficult to apply evenly, especially with a brush. If you brush on the dye, more tends to soak into the wood where you first touch it with the bristles. When the wood does take up the stain unevenly the surface acquires an interesting blotchy, textured feel which can be appealing in its own right.

A clean, lint-free cloth often proves a more satisfactory means of applying a smooth coat of stain. The pad absorbs the runny stain and distributes it evenly, especially into the crevices of carved and turned wood. Alternatively, a sponge paint pad is a good way of getting consistent cover, except in tight corners.

The wood itself has to be protected by wax polish, oil or clear varnish after using this type of stain. When you prepare the wood thoroughly in the first place and apply several coats of varnish over the stained timbers, the finish should be robust enough to withstand wear-and-tear for many years.

Semi-translucent paint displays the grain like a stain, allowing the natural beauty of the timber to show through, but instead of wood tones it comes in a range of pale pastel colours. A combination of chalky green, blue and white produces a

▲ **Emerging shadows**
Even after staining in pale grey, the grain in the wood of these display units and drawers is clearly visible. Fascinating shadows in the timber emerge from the stain, conveying a worn look that is totally compatible with a matured country kitchen.

cool, refreshing impression; misty pink and peach add a warmer, comforting touch.

The paint is easy to apply and protects woodwork with a tough, low-sheen coating that is quick to clean and resistant to damage. Brush it on evenly in the direction of the grain and leave to dry for at least six hours before re-applying; two coats are recommended. For good results, this paint needs to be applied to a new light-coloured or stripped wood in which a strong fingerprint of the grain is evident.

Exterior stains Special microporous sealers or stains must be used on external woodwork.

Applying wood stains

Whatever type of stain you decide to use it is important to do a test first on an inconspicuous spot to check the colour. The result depends on the colour and grain of the original wood and how much of the stain it absorbs. Remember also that further coats of stain will deepen the colour. So let the first coat be absorbed and test a smaller area with another coat on top. You can mix stain colours of the same type to achieve the shade you prefer.

You should also test the effect of the final finish you intend to use over the stain; most waxes and oils tend to darken surfaces while even clear varnish contributes a yellowish hue.

---

tip

Quick dyes
Cold water fabric dye powders diluted in water are fine for staining small areas and even better if you want a faded, worn look. Since they are not specifically designed for use on wood they tend to fade further in direct sunlight.

▼ **Accumulating colour**
The gradation of shades in these panelled shutters is achieved by working down the panels, giving each board one more coat of the same coloured wood stain than its neighbour above.

◄ **Grizzled grain**
Staining small wooden items of furniture like this free-standing towel rail grants them a peculiar distinction. The mottled effect of colour-stained wood blends particularly effectively with the blotchiness on colour-washed walls.

◄ **Outdoor shades**
These lovely bright stain colours pick out the decorative details of an unusual plant trough for the garden. It's a good idea to choose your flowers to complement the colour scheme.

► **Step by step**
Alternating bands of natural and colour stained boards in a random fashion creates an intriguing individual pattern on the floor.

Preparing the surface
Untreated, light wood shows off the colours best. Previously painted or varnished wood should be stripped thoroughly before applying a fresh finish. Fill any blemishes with wood filler. Make sure all surfaces are sanded to a nearly smooth finish, dry and free from dust and wax.

The same goes for wood floors as well. Usually you will need to hire a sander to smooth the surface and remove any old paint and stain. Rub down the surface with white spirit.

Materials
Rubber gloves
Old saucer or **shallow container**
Clean, lint-free cloths
Fine glasspaper

USING WOOD STAIN

1 Taking care Wear rubber gloves to avoid staining your fingers. Decant some of the stain from the can into an old saucer or shallow container, so that you can judge how much the cloth soaks up each time it is dipped into the dye.

2 Putting on the stain Take a clean, lint-free rag folded into a pad and dip it into the stain. Pressing lightly and evenly, apply a thin coat of stain to the wood, working with the grain. Work swiftly without a pause to avoid patchiness. Then quickly wipe over with a clean cloth to pick up any excess.

3 Completing the finish Allow to dry – a couple of hours for a water-based stain, at least 6 hours for an oil-based one. If the finish is too light apply a second coat in the same way; if the finish is too dark lightly sand the surface.

Stencilling with wood stains
After staining a surface in one colour to serve as a base coat, you can use wood stains in other shades to stencil a pattern on to it. Carefully done in various woody tones, this creates a convincing marquetry-like result which can look very mellow and individual. Worked out in brighter colours, you can stencil a rug on the floor or a cloth on a table; patterns picked out in pastel shade look good on bedroom floors and furniture. Running a stencilled border around the fringes of the floor clearly defines its boundaries, especially when teamed with a co-ordinated skirting and a central rug in toning colours.
Quick brush patterns Using a thin paint brush dipped in stain of a darker tone you can casually apply lines and squiggles of pattern to stained timber for an impromptu design.

◀ *Stain stencils*
Executing an ambitious stencilled pattern in coloured stains on plain door panels produces a magnificent result and transforms ordinary pine dresser and cupboard units into a treasured family heirloom.

Stripping wood

Old timber furniture, varnished, polished or oiled to a soft sheen, is very much part of the traditional country look. But all too often the beauty of the wood has been lost under layers of scuffed paint or hard, darkened varnish. These need to be stripped away before the wood beneath is exposed in its original glory. The time and trouble spent resurrecting an immaculate piece of furniture from behind a dilapidated exterior can be tremendously fulfilling.

Checking the finish
It is important to know what the finish is before you start to sand, clean or chemically strip it, since methods vary.

Painted finish Usually a glance at the back, underneath or inside of the drawers or doors reveals the nature and quality of the timber beneath. Old pine furniture has often been painted in the past. You need to remove the paint with a chemical stripper.

Doors and less valuable pine furniture can be commercially stripped in baths of caustic soda, which saves time and effort but has disadvantages. Old glues are dissolved by the process so that the sections of the furniture can come apart. Also, the grain of the wood is raised when the caustic soda is washed off and careful sanding is necessary to restore the surface. Remember to remove fittings before immersion.

▼▶ **From ugly duckling to swan**
All the effort and attention lavished on this chair is rewarded when a delightfully mellow wood hatches from beneath the scruffy surface.

Blow lamps and hot air strippers are best avoided as there is a danger of scorching the wood.

Varnish Old varnishes are usually very dark in colour; alternatively a modern clear polyurethane varnish may have been used. If you are not sure whether a piece of furniture has been varnished do a quick test to check. Clean the surface with reviving fluid (see page 58). If the surface does not respond to this treatment, then it has probably been varnished. Varnish has to be removed with chemical stripper or a hard surface remover.

Veneered furniture Wood veneer is a fine layer of a quality wood such as walnut or maple which has been glued to the surfaces of a cheaper wood like pine. It is important to check if an item is veneered, as it can be easily damaged or partially removed if handled roughly. The bottom edges of drawers and doors will often provide the necessary information but if these are covered with paint you will need to scrape away a section so that you can study the wood more closely.

It is best to hand-sand a finish gently on veneered furniture but this is hard and very time consuming if the furniture has been painted or varnished. In this case, use chemical stripper gel or paste and remove the paint in thin layers, taking great care not to scratch the surface as you peel the stripper away.

Waxed or oiled furniture This usually responds to cleaning with a reviving fluid but if you wish to change the colour of the wood or the finish you will need to remove it completely. Sanding is the best method. First use a medium then a fine glasspaper and work with the grain of the wood. When you are back to bare wood give the surface a final rub with very fine 000 grade wire wool. On very large surfaces you can use an orbital sander to do most of the work but the final rubbing down should always be done by hand.

Types of chemical stripper

Liquid, gel or paste strippers react with paint and varnish, softening it so that the paint becomes easy to scrape off. In all cases, test a little of the paint stripper on a concealed patch of the furniture to check how long you will need to leave the stripper to work and if it causes any unwanted discolouration in the wood.

Remember to remove any metal or ceramic knobs or hinges before you use the chemical stripper as these can be damaged by the chemicals in the stripper. Wooden handles are also best removed and stripped separately.

Liquid or gel strippers may be water or spirit based. On furniture it is best to use a spirit-based stripper as this will not raise the grain of the wood as water does, so you won't have to sand the surface smooth again.

Check the manufacturer's advice. As a guideline, if water is recommended for washing down the wood after stripping then the stripper is water based; if however white spirit or methylated spirits is used to wash down the wood instead, the stripper is spirit based.

Paste stripper is ideal for use on carved or turned wood like chair backs and banisters.

Materials
Rubber gloves
Old paint brush for applying the liquid or gel
Trowel or **old palette knife** for spreading the paste
Liquid, gel or **paste stripper**
Flat scraper and **shave hook** for smoothly paring away the softened paint
White spirit or **water** and a clean **cloth** for rinsing off the stripper
Fine grade glasspaper and **fine wire wool, 000 grade,** for rubbing and buffing down

USING CHEMICAL STRIPPER

Liquid and gel strippers It is best to apply gel strippers with a paint brush. When blisters appear on the surface, strip off the softened finish with a scraper, using a shave hook or old nail file for crevices and carvings. You may need to apply several coats of stripper if there are a number of layers of paint to remove.

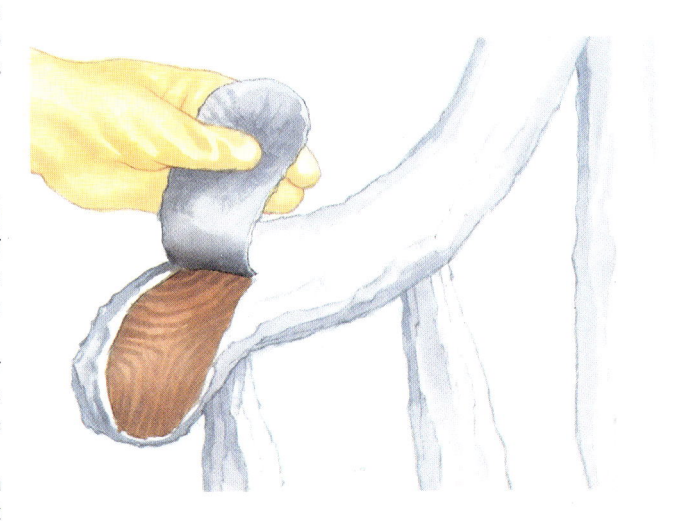

Paste stripper Mix the powder with water to form a thick paste according to the manufacturer's instructions. Apply thickly with a trowel and leave for about 30 minutes. Then peel away in strips. Rinse with a damp cloth to neutralize.

If there are several layers of paint you may need to leave the paste on longer. To prevent the paste stripper drying out, cover and bind the pasted areas with sheets or strips of polythene; you could use old polythene bags for this. The paste will liquefy the paint and sometimes this will run down on to the floor.

Always stand the furniture on several thicknesses of newspaper covered with a dust sheet or, if stripping items like banisters, remove carpeting or other floor coverings as it can work out expensive if you have to buy new carpets too.

Re-finishing
Once the old finish has been removed the surface will probably need sanding smooth and then bleaching and filling if necessary before the final protective surface is applied to the wood.

Wood bleaches

Sometimes stripping off the existing finish reveals stains in the wood which can be removed with a proprietary wood bleach. This is useful, too, for lightening the natural colour of the wood so you can apply a lighter coloured stain. After bleaching you will need to sand down the surface since the process usually raises the grain of the wood.

You can either use oxalic acid crystals (see page 60) or a proprietary solution, which comes in two bottles that are applied separately but work in conjunction when used according to the manufacturer's instructions.

Materials
Proprietary wood bleach, 2 glass jars and an **old paint brush**
White vinegar and a **bucket** and **cloth**

BLEACHING WOOD

1 Priming the surface Pour the first solution into a clean, empty jam jar. Apply generously to the surface with an old paint brush and leave for 10 minutes. The wood may darken slightly as it soaks in.

2 Mixing on the surface Brush on the second solution and leave it for several hours or overnight. Remove any scum that appears with a scrubbing brush and clean water.

3 Rinsing off the bleach Wipe over the surface with a half-and-half mixture of white vinegar and water. This treatment raises the grain which will need sanding to smoothness again.

Grain filling

Even the most finely planed and sanded wood is full of minute cracks and pores which deflect the light in different directions, dulling the surface. Using a grain filler makes the surface more reflective and therefore glossier.

Materials
Very fine glasspaper, grain filler and **white spirit**
2 lint-free cloths and **wood dye**

FILLING THE GRAIN

1 Rubbing down Sand the surface in the direction of the grain with very fine glasspaper.

2 Mixing the filler Dilute the grain filler to a thin paste with white spirit.

3 Smoothing a loose grain Apply the filler to the surface with a cloth, rubbing in across the grain. Remove excess filler using a clean cloth. Leave overnight to harden.

paint brush

palette knife

fine glasspaper

cloth

Varnishing wood

As one of the most hardwearing and easy-to-apply finishes, polyurethane varnish can be clear or tinted to simulate real wood colours, with a gloss, silk or matt look. Modern varnishes must only be applied to surfaces which are free from dirt, grease, oil and wax (see page 58).

Coloured varnish or varnish stains are varnishes which have been coloured with dyes or translucent pigments. They are easier to put on than stain on its own and provides protection at the same time. As the colour is brushed on with the varnish each coat slightly deepens the tone.

When using polyurethane varnish on bare wood, it is usually advisable to thin the first coat so that it soaks in quickly and seals the grain. Solvent-based polyurethanes are thinned with white spirit, according to the manufacturer's instructions, and generally applied with a cloth to avoid minute bubbles forming in the surface. Afterwards, the sealed wood can be sanded and finished with further coats of full strength varnish or wax polished for a more natural finish.

Wash the brushes in white spirits and set them aside specifically for varnishing in the future.

APPLYING VARNISH

1 Wiping on the first coat Using a diluted varnish and a clean cloth, wipe over the surface to seal it.

2 Varnishing Apply the varnish along the grain first, drawing the brush backwards and forwards. Don't overload the brush. Dip it in the varnish and touch the ends of the bristles against the side of the tin; don't scrape the bristles across the lip as this tends to create bubbles in the finished work.

▲ **Aftercare**
Once the wood has been stripped and sanded it is important to treat it with a clear varnish, wood stain or a wax finish. Varnish stains protect the timber.

3 Brushing on the final coat Using light pressure, brush at right angles across the grain. Then finish off along the grain as lightly as possible using the tip of the brush.

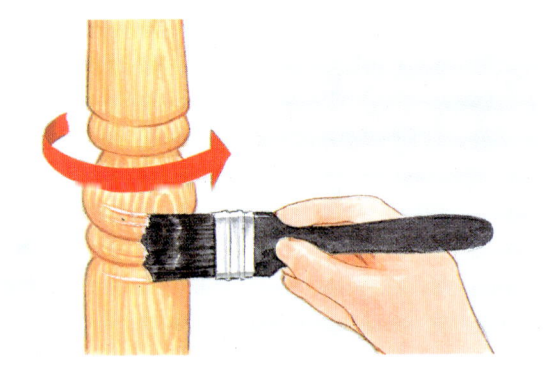

4 Working on turned wood When varnishing stair or chair spindles work round the pattern this will keep the effect even. On mouldings, work only along the grain to avoid major drips and runs.

tip

Applying varnish stain
Apply a first thin coat with a cloth so that it seals the wood's surface. When this is dry lightly sand to remove any bubbles or brush bristles in the finish. Then apply further coats with a brush. Remember that the colour will deepen slightly when each coat is applied.

Reviving old furniture

Over the years, old timber furniture becomes discoloured and lacklustre. Dusting and polishing protect the timber but also rub in dirt that eventually obscures all sign of the timber grain. Cleaning the surface to remove this accumulated grime takes only an hour or so and allows all the original beauty of the wood to glow through again.

The great advantage of this gentle cleaning is that it preserves all the hard labour of the original craftsman and the sheen provided by previous owners' care. Treat valuable pieces of furniture especially tenderly; antique renovation is a delicate business, probably best left to experts. Also be careful when treating veneers; too much water or liquid cleaner will lift the surface. Choose a gel or paste as this does not soak in too far or need much washing down after use.

▼ **A warm glow**
Particles of smoke from an open fire can tarnish wood, but gentle cleaning restores its natural radiance.

Cleaning and reviving the finish
Special proprietary timber cleaners and revivers that dissolve away old wax, lacquer, oil and traditional varnishes and replenish the oils of the dried out wood are available from hardware stores. If you decide to use one of these, follow the manufacturer's instructions.

To make your own reviver you will need equal quantities of raw linseed oil and white spirit; an eggcupful of each should be sufficient for most items of furniture. Add to this mixture a drop or two of vinegar. Place the ingredients in a screw top bottle and shake to mix well. Do not use this mixture on light wood as it can darken the surface, or on a crazed finish as the oil will seep deep into the cracked areas giving a blotched finish.

CLEANING THE SURFACE

Always test the cleaning solution on a small inconspicuous area first, to ensure that the wood and cleaner are compatible and that you like the appearance of the wood after cleaning. Resist the temptation to overclean the surface and risk wiping away the character of ageing.

Materials
Old newspapers or **dust cloths**.
Rubber gloves.
Linseed oil, **white spirit** and **vinegar** or **Proprietary wood reviver**
Lint-free cloth, **old toothbrush** and **very fine wire wool grade 000**.

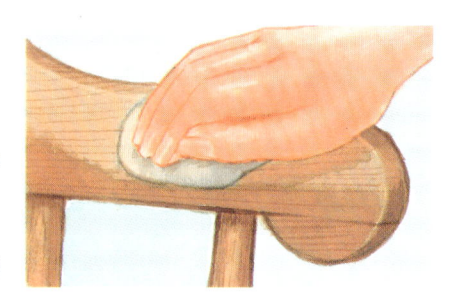

1 Dislodging the dirt Rub the mixture on to the furniture with a soft cloth in a circular movement. This will remove the surface finish and grime; at first it will become sticky and dirty as the old finish is released, so constantly re-fold or replace the cloth until the finish no longer comes off. Complete by rubbing with the direction of the grain to clean this out.

2 Cleaning in awkward places For carved areas or mouldings use a soft toothbrush to get into the crevices. A small pointed tool like a toothpick, cocktail stick or cotton bud is handy for digging the dirt out of deep, narrow grooves. Don't use a metal pick as this might scratch or mark the wood.

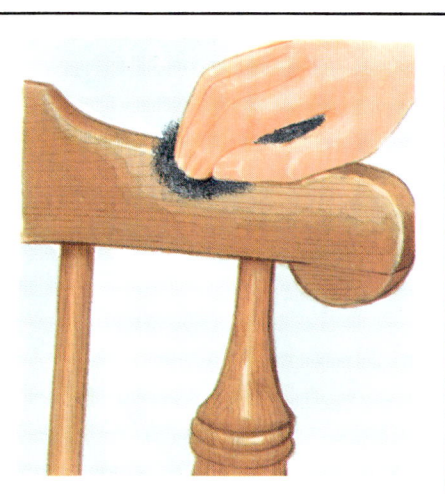

3 Shifting stubborn dirt If the surface proves difficult to remove use very fine wire wool, grade 000, instead of a cloth. Moisten with the cleaning solution and rub lightly to ensure that you do not scratch the surface. End by rubbing with the grain. Wipe up the dislodged grime as you work.

tip

Stripping the finish
Always start by attempting to clean any piece of old furniture before you resort to the much more drastic step of chemically stripping it. If cleaning has no effect it probably means that the wood has a cellulose lacquer or a polyurethane varnished finish. Stripping will then be necessary before you can apply a new finish. On cellulose lacquer use a cellulose thinner to lubricate the surface well, rub away at it until it becomes sticky and then wipe off. Finally clean the surface with methylated spirits. Use a spirit based stripper or hard finish remover to get rid of the varnish.

Repairing blemishes

Having removed the dirt, assess the state of the wood and the amount of damage before re-polishing. Superficial blemishes in the finish can usually be removed or disguised with a few simple materials and a little elbow-grease.

TREATING SCRATCHES

Materials
Old newspapers or **dust cloths**.
Wood scratch remover crayon.
Flour paper or **fine glasspaper**.
Linseed oil.
Soft cloth.
Wood filler and **filling knife**.

Curing fine scratches Try rubbing out fine surface scratching with flour paper or very fine glasspaper dipped in a little linseed oil. Sometimes you may only notice this delicate crackling when you are polishing for the first time in a while. Wait and see what nourishing effect the wax has on the surface before taking any further action.

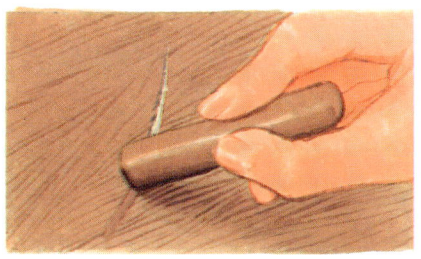

Disguising light scratches A special wax furniture crayon comes in a range of colours to match wood tones and is available from most hardware stores. Carefully rub the crayon back and forth along the line of the scratch. Then, using a soft cloth, rub over the surface to ensure the crayon filling ends up flush with the surrounding wood.

▶ **Unveiling the wood**
Fortunately, the individual signature of the grain in fine furniture can easily be uncovered from beneath a layer of darkening dirt. With careful, mild treatment, all the original lustre of the timber is brought to light again.

TREATING WOODWORM

The first thing to look for when buying any second-hand items of wooden furniture at an auction or from a junk shop is woodworm. If this is not dealt with other timber in the house can become infested.

Woodworm is the larva of the woodwork beetle which remains in the wood, tunnelling its way around and eating the timber until it emerges as a beetle up to five years later.

Always search for any sign of the characteristic little holes before taking old furniture into your home. Never buy furniture riddled with woodworm; badly-infested wood will be soft, even to the point of weakness. Mild cases can be treated.

Materials
Rubber gloves.
Old newspapers or dust cloths.
Woodworm-killing fluid.
Wood filler.
Filling knife.

1 Check furniture for tiny holes As well as looking on all the obvious surfaces, hunt carefully over the underside and back. If you find holes this does not necessarily mean the woodworm is still active. Old holes often have a dark lining while fresh ones are lighter. Tap the furniture to see if any dust appears from the holes. A fine sand-like dust is an indication of recent activity.

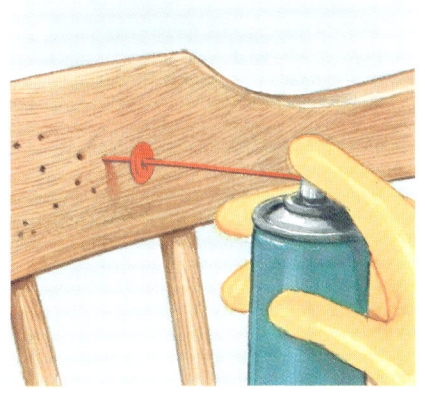

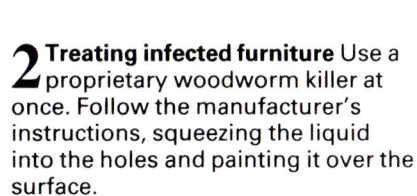

2 Treating infected furniture Use a proprietary woodworm killer at once. Follow the manufacturer's instructions, squeezing the liquid into the holes and painting it over the surface.

3 Sealing the holes Plug the small woodworm holes with wood filler. Use a filler blade to press it into the cavities. Allow to dry before lightly sanding off to a smooth finish with fine glasspaper.

Filling cracks and holes These should be filled with proprietary wood filler in a colour that matches the colour of the timber. Use a flexible blade filling knife; an old palette knife is a good alternative.

Bedding in Press the filler into the crack or hole so that it stands slightly higher than the surrounding surface to allow for shrinkage as it dries. When completely dry, sand level to the rest of the surface.

Dealing with burn marks First rub over the patch with fine glasspaper to remove the charring. Then use scratch cover to build up the finish again; this may always show, but less obviously than the burn mark.

59

REMOVING RINGS

Materials
Rubber gloves.
Old newspapers or dust cloths.
White spirit.
Wire wool, grade 000 and soft cloth.
Flour paper or very fine glasspaper.

Caused by heat or water, white rings only affect the finish on the wood and can usually be removed using white spirit and small pad of very fine, 000 grade wire wool.

Dip the steel wool in a little white spirit in a saucer, then, following the grain of the wood, rub it over the mark. If the stain is not removed try damping it with white spirit then rubbing the stain gently using a very fine glasspaper. You may need to repeat this, lubricating the area with white spirit each time.

If neither of these methods works, try reviving the finish following the instructions for cleaning the surface. If this does not remove the mark the surface will need stripping and then re-polishing.

BLEACHING INK MARKS

Materials
Rubber gloves.
Old newspapers or dust cloths.
Oxalic acid crystals or wood bleach.
Fine artist's paint brush.
Cotton wool.

Common on old desks and tables, ink stains can be bleached out using oxalic acid crystals. These are available from pharmacists. Oxalic acid is poisonous so label it well and lock it away. Dissolve one tablespoon of the crystals in two tablespoons of boiling water.

Then, wearing rubber gloves, apply the mixture on a pad of cotton wool or with a small paint brush. Leave in place for a few minutes before dabbing at the mark. Clean off with dry cotton wool to soak up remaining acid. Repeat if necessary. You can also use a proprietary two-part wood bleach, in which case follow the manufacturer's instructions.

REMOVING DENTS

Materials
Boiling water.
Warm iron.
Damp cloth.

Water raises the grain on wood and is therefore normally avoided when working on timber. However there is one occasion, for removing a dent, when this problem can be advantageous. This treatment is not suitable for veneered wood.

For a small dent Apply a few drops of boiling water to the dent to make the fibres of the wood swell. Leave to allow the wood to dry completely before polishing.

For a large dent Lay a damp cloth over the area and press with the tip of a heated iron. Be careful not to scorch the surface; don't use a very hot iron or leave it there too long.

RE-FINISHING THE SURFACE

Waxed polished surface To bring back the lustre to a previously wax polished surface that has been cleaned and revived you will only need to re-polish it. Use a good quality wax polish and just wipe the cloth across the surface of the polish lightly. This will provide enough wax to polish two or three small pieces of furniture or one large one. Dust regularly and re-apply every two months or so.

Oiled surface Use a proprietary furniture oil sparingly, rubbing just a little well into the surface with a vigorous movement, working along the grain. Allow to dry for an hour before buffing to a lustrous finish with a clean, lint-free cloth like cotton stockinette. Repeat every six months to build up a tough, stain-resistant surface.

tip

Safety precautions
Protect your surroundings When treating any furniture, always spread out plenty of old newspapers or dust cloths under and around the area.
Open air Make sure the room is well ventilated or work out of doors – a garage is ideal.
Do not smoke around inflammable materials.
Wear old clothes and rubber gloves to shield your skin from caustic solutions.
Read the maker's instructions on any chemicals before starting work.
Store safely Be sure to keep all chemicals well out of the reach of children.

Turn to stone

Ever since the fourteenth century, stone and brick have been among the most important materials for building houses. Local stone produced distinctive regional characteristics, by determining a building's construction as well as the colour and texture of its walls. Houses in the Cotswolds are renowned for being constructed from smooth blocks of golden limestone, while rugged cottages in Wales are built of granite boulders and roofed with slate tiles, giving them an affinity with their surroundings.

In places where stone was hard to quarry or unavailable, bricks were used instead. Again, the type of clay found in an area produced bricks of a particular shade of red, giving the local building a distinctive hue. As brick-making developed, the choice of colours widened and, by the eighteenth century, grey and brown bricks were favoured for more fashionable houses.

Today, natural stone and brick are valued for their stylish qualities inside the house as well as out, but this wasn't always the case. Rooms in medieval and Tudor houses were almost always plastered, limewashed and then painted with a decorative design. Paradoxically, these early paint finishes would often mimic ashlar stone, as precision-cut blocks laid regularly with fine joints between them.

At ground level

Before the seventeenth century, floors, at least at ground level, were laid with flagstones or beaten earth in humbler dwellings. These basic materials gave way later to brick, tile and eventually to timber, while the old, hard surfaces survived only in the kitchen.

The inglenook fireplace that heated the main living area of most older houses was often built of crude stone or brick. As fire openings became smaller, they acquired decorative surrounds, made from materials like marble and carved stone, that remain the focal point of every country sitting room.

▶ **The passage of time**
Dark grey local slate makes a handsome and practical flooring in this ancient Welsh country cottage. Over the years its well-trodden surface has gradually worn to a gleaming shine. Left uncovered, it blends happily with the other natural textures to create a cool, rustic atmosphere.

▲ **Cook's choice**
A slab of polished black marble set into this work surface contrasts dramatically with the primrose-coloured units, and provides the perfect work surface.

▼ **Cold comfort**
Although stone is a naturally cool surface, its colours can be surprisingly warm. The comparison between the wall and floor in this cottage shows how polish enriches coloration.

Building with stone

Because stone and slate so often form the fabric of a building, it's hardly surprising that they dominate the major interior surfaces as well. Flagstones, stone walls and exposed brick have a natural integrity and permanence that make them the perfect backdrop for robust, solid country furniture and pretty floral fabrics.

Floors

Flags cut from slate and all kinds of limestone and sandstone are the natural flooring materials commonly found in old houses. Years of wear make virtually no impression on cool, dark slate, which can be sawn and polished to a smooth finish or split to give a wonderfully rippled surface.

Sandstone and limestone vary in colour from light blonde to brown and grey. They are much softer than slate, so in older houses their surfaces will often have been worn into gentle contours over the years. This usually only adds to their charm and need not be remedied unless it presents a hazard underfoot.

Although they are man-made, brick and tiles often have the same natural look as stone and slate. Laid in herringbone, basket weave or checker-board patterns, their russet tones and grainy textures have a friendly warmth.

Stone and slate should be regularly swept and occasionally scrubbed to keep them clean. Smooth stones can be buffed to a shine with an electric floor polisher. If you prefer a glossy finish and want to prevent dirt from becoming ingrained in the porous surface, stone, brick and terracotta tiles can be sealed by brushing with boiled linseed oil then, when it has been absorbed, finishing with a wax floor polish.

Walls

Rough stone walls and exposed brickwork have a great appeal in a country-style home. However, since their natural colour and pattern is so dominant, in most cases it is probably wise to restrict them to a specific part of the room, such as a chimney breast.

If you suspect that beautiful stone or brick lies beneath the plasterwork in any of the rooms in your home, you may want to expose it. Remember, however, that the builder is unlikely to have used the finest materials or spent much time on the finish of the work, knowing it was soon to be hidden by plaster.

Stone walls look best left in their natural state. If dust becomes a problem, it can be laid by coating the surface with a matt sealant. To prevent dust lodging on the uneven surface of stone and brick, dust it with a brush attachment fitted to the vacuum cleaner.

Fireplaces

In most houses, the traditional place for displaying the stone mason's skill is round the fireplace. Inglenook fireplaces may sometimes have a carved stone lintel over the fire opening. Smaller fireplaces might have a surround and hearth made from grey or beige sandstone. The black marks left on the stone by soot, falling coals or logs are very difficult to shift, but add character to the hearth.

In grand houses, fire surrounds were very often made from marble which came in beautiful glowing colours, as well as black and white. It could be carved into exquisitely intricate decorations or quite restrained classical designs.

▲ **Inside and out**
Traditional houses were often built of the same stone throughout, to give a sense of continuity and an impression of space and elegance. The flagstones in this lobby blend beautifully with its mellow Cotswold's stone walls. In fact, the walls of this house look very similar from the outside as well, linking the interior firmly with its surroundings.

▶ **Cue for colour**
Marble comes in many colours other than the familiar black-and-white veined varieties. This beautiful brown marble needed no enhancement, so the fireplace was carved with just a pair of classical corbels to support the mantelshelf. Note how the colour of the painted dado panelling echoes the tan-coloured stone.

▲ **Take to the water**
Cool, clean marble is the perfect material for a bath surround. It shrugs off water and conveys the nostalgic appearance of a luxurious, old-fashioned bathroom.

▼ **Rock solid**
Laminated worktops may not be as prestigious as polished stone ones, but they are equally practical. Here, the pinky grey mock granite surfaces co-ordinate well with the bricks.

Introducing stone

In newer houses, where stone rarely features as an interior surface, many of the existing hard materials, like ceramic and vinyl tiles, plaster and laminate surfaces, can be replaced by real stone, to give the home a traditional look.

One reason for the demise of stone as a building material was the difficulty of finding craftsmen who were sufficiently skilled in stone-masonry. Nowadays, slate, marble and granite are available in the form of practical and inexpensive tiles, which can be laid as flooring or hung as wallcoverings instead of ceramic tiles. Larger slate and stone flags can still be bought, and although they are more expensive initially they will last indefinitely.

Exposed brickwork is popular in country-style kitchens. Builders will often include a partition wall, chimney breast or extractor hood as a feature of the design. The use of secondhand bricks will give the new construction an established look. If these prove hard to find, new ones that have a mottled, aged effect can be very convincing.

On the face of it

Facing stones are sometimes applied to a plastered wall to give it the appearance of natural brick or stone, but use these with care. Any material that is out of character with the house will rarely blend comfortably with any of the surrounding features.

Imitations of natural materials should not necessarily be dismissed out of hand. Some make a real contribution to the style you are trying to create. Laminated kitchen worktops, for example, come in realistic copies of granite, slate and marble, and are as practical as they are good looking.

Secondhand benefits

If you are after the real thing in terms of both material and age, architectural salvage centres can be fruitful hunting grounds. You might find marble slabs, fire surrounds or worn flagstones that, when transplanted into your home, will provide an instant venerability.

It may take weeks or months to track down the materials you need. Always carry a note of any vital dimensions in case you come across an unexpected find. When buying building materials secondhand, it's safe to ignore minor blemishes but be wary of incomplete fireplaces, crumbling stone and other, supposedly bargain buys that might require expensive restoration.

Keep an open mind, too. Items that were designed for one specific purpose might adapt well to a new role. A marble top salvaged from a worm-eaten washstand might be fixed to the wall behind a washbasin as a splashback, and a couple of balustrades from a garden terrace could be brought indoors to support a sheet of plate glass as a hall table.

▲ **Table talk**
Veined, marble-topped tables look lovely in a conservatory, on a patio or in a sunny kitchen, but take care how you treat them. The surface can be marked by oil or acid, and will chip if knocked.

▼ **Slated floor**
Originally, slate slab floors were built into the structure of old buildings. Nowadays, there are easy-to-lay slate tiles available, which will create a similar effect in a modern house at less cost than real flagstones.

◄ **Painted panels**
Here, marble painting combines with other paint effects to produce a formal look with an amusing twist of fun.

These trompe l'oeil marble panels in a dado are outlined so that they appear to be recessed in a background of yellow dragging. Such a lively, sunny idea can be used very effectively to brighten up a dining room, hallway or staircase.

Painting the skirting with a marbled effect to match will add an extra flourish to the theme. If there is already a marble feature in the room, its colour and grain can be copied in the painting.

▼ **Make-believe marble**
The simple shape of this wooden fireplace makes it an ideal subject for a first attempt at marble painting. It is much easier to create a flow in the pattern of the grain if there is no intricate carving to contend with. This white-and-black-on-grey colouring is also one of the simplest to reproduce.

Once you have mastered the basic technique, there is no need to imitate genuine marble. Even though the variety of colours and patterns in natural marble offers infinite inspiration, you can achieve some exciting fantasy effects using your own choice of colours.

Stone effects

Where the look of stone is more important than its texture, strength or durability, painted faux finishes can give exactly the right impression. With the current interest in paint effects, it is no longer difficult to find a decorator with the skill to mimic masonry or marble.

Expertly done, marble-painting looks very convincing and can be used to decorate fireplaces, dados, pillars, bath-side panels, walls and even floors. For a realistic effect, only surfaces that could be made from real marble should be painted with a marble-like finish. If you want to camouflage a fixture like a modern radiator or built-in cupboard, these too can be painted to match a marble-painted wall behind.

The advantage of painted finishes over real stone or marble is that they can be changed when you redecorate. The natural materials come in so many variations of colour and pattern that inspiration will never be lacking. You can change from marble to granite or pink sandstone to alter the mood and the colour scheme.

Apart from decorating the room itself, painted stone effects will give extra weight and substance to furniture and accessories. Lamp bases, mirror frames, bathroom cabinets and dressing-table tops are just a few of the surfaces that would benefit from a mock-stone finish. The object need not be valuable, but it should be an attractive shape and one that could feasibly be made from the material it imitates. Small-scale projects like these are an ideal introduction to the technique, before progressing to larger items and areas.

Tile style

An imaginative use of tiling in your kitchen or bathroom can cleverly combine sensible practicality with design flair. From a functional point of view, ceramic tiles are tough, resistant to water, steam, heat and staining and make an ideal covering in any location where a wipeable surface is desirable.

The tiles may be glazed or unglazed, patterned or plain, and vary greatly in size, shape and thickness. For the adventurous and creative, there is a huge range of vibrant colours; plus decorative patterns and textures in period, regional or contemporary styles. In addition there are narrow borders and richly decorated mural and panel effects, from which to choose. You will find good selections in home decorating stores, builder's and plumber's merchants, supermarkets, department stores and from specialist tile centres.

Costings

Tiles do vary in price, but tiling is not necessarily the most expensive method of covering any surface. You will need to balance the initial outlay against their practical advantages, decorative effect and subsequent low redecorating costs.

Ordinary white and neutral tiles are generally less expensive than ones in vivid hues, original patterns or handmade tiles. If you are tempted by anything particularly vibrant or unusual, be sure you won't tire of the finished result, as a mistake will be costly to rectify. Try to be open-ended in your original selection, so that the tiles will adapt readily when it comes to refurbishing.

Plain and patterned

If you want to keep costs down, stylish design effects can be produced by an enterprising use of plain tiles. On their own, a wall of cleverly positioned plain tiles can be subtly pleasing. Square and rectangular tiles can be laid stepped, in bricklaying fashion, while square tiles laid diagonally make a considerable design impact.

Plain tiles can also be combined with decorative ones, run as borders or interspersed as single motif tiles, panels or a tiled mural. Remember, if you use tiles from different ranges, check that they are of equal thickness.

▲ **Spoilt for choice**
As this dazzling array of tiles demonstrates, tiling can be a very creative experience. Such a welter of sizes, exciting patterns and lively colours can be very inspiring, although maybe initially a little daunting, too, when it comes to deciding on the final selection.

Tiles in kitchens

Ceramic tiles are an ideal covering for worktops and splashbacks because they are robust and durable enough to withstand the brunt of most cooking activities and be quickly wiped clean again to prevent them becoming shabby or grubby.

While most ordinary ceramic tiles can be used as work surfaces, tiles manufactured especially for this purpose will last longer. Quarry tiles, designed as a floorcovering, are not suitable, unless they are sealed. Even though worktop and quarry tiles are thicker than ordinary ceramic wall tiles, they can be fixed to a wall to create a co-ordinated splashback. Thick, hand-finished ceramic tiles, with their pleasing individual variations of colour and pattern, look very attractive with pale or dark wood fitted units and give the kitchen a suitably country feel.

Tiles can be laid over an existing, possibly scratched or worn, work surface, but you must check first whether the existing worktop is strong enough to take their weight. The tiles must always be laid on to a flat surface, otherwise they will crack.

On the down side, tiled work surfaces can be noisy to work on, and individual tiles can be chipped or cracked if something heavy is accidentally dropped on it. But generally, when treated with respect, a tiled worktop is hard-wearing and long lasting.

Visually, a colourful or highly patterned tiled splashback can become the focus of the kitchen. Either the splashback or the worktop should dominate the scene, without fighting each other for prominence. So a bright splashback is best set against a plain or pale worktop, and vice versa, to avoid creating a working area that is too loud.

▲ **White out**
A wall-full of easy-to-clean white tiles is a good way of ensuring a fresh, bright look in a kitchen.

▼ **Two by two**
A splashback made of odd pairs of hand-finished tiles is delightfully sympathetic to the old-fashioned character of this kitchen.

▶ **Farmyard characters**
A tiled wall, decorated with charming little farm animals, dictates the fresh colour scheme of this country-style kitchen. You could give a plain white tiled wall a similar and completely new look by painting ducks, hens, cockerels, goats, dogs and horses on to the tiles with stencils and ceramic paints.

Fitting tiles

Before you let your imagination run away with you, however, you should sort out the practicalities. Start by examining the shape and size of your room, work out a design scheme in some detail and assess how many plain or patterned tiles you will need.

Look out for ranges which include curved edging tiles for a neat finish. Some manufacturers produce mitred edging for the corners. Alternatively, a wooden edging strip will frame worktop tiling. You can also find right-angle tiles to continue the work surface smoothly up the wall behind. Failing that, you can buy quadrant-shaped tiles to fill the angle between the wall and worktop.

Tiling can be a satisfying activity. However, if you have any doubts about your tiling prowess, you would be well advised to employ an expert, because bad tiling looks dreadful.

▲ **Display panels**
Two posturing cockerels boldly face up to each other behind the hob. In this case, rather than using individual motifs, each image is assembled by matching up six separate tiles in jigsaw fashion. Positioned prominently like this, tiled panels become quite an eye-catching feature of the room. When selecting the plain tiles to go with the patterned ones, make sure they are of a compatible size and the same thickness.

Tiles in bathrooms

Ceramic tiles have long been recognized as one of the most practical surfaces for a bathroom. Being non-absorbent, they help to contend with the problems caused by condensation. Steam billowing from a running hot-water tap creates a high humidity that can eventually make the wallpaper peel and paint flake. In fact, a mixer tap that runs hot and cold water together, prevents clouds of steam forming in the first place.

In recent years, the options for the creative use of tiles have expanded rapidly with the burgeoning choice of styles. Some manufacturers produce tiles that match the colours of standard bathroom ware which allows you to create a co-ordinated scheme; this is useful in small spaces where a unified colour scheme is desirable. These co-ordinating ranges are often plain but can be marbled, speckled or textured. They also provide a neutral background for inserting patterned or relief tiles.

◄ **Out of the blue**
In this bathroom, a three tile system of one heavily and one lightly patterned tile with a matching half-tile has been laid to produce an all-over, co-ordinated effect.

► **Dado designs**
Inserting a dado band of narrow coloured tiles is an excellent way of jazzing up a bland expanse of plain tiling. Dividing the wall up like this gives the room a definite structure. Here, motif tiles are alternated with all-white ones below the dado level to create a regular pattern. The design could easily be made more haphazard by interspersing the patterned tiles irregularly.

◀ **Patchwork of tiles**
Instead of opting for a ready made, cohesive look, shop around for individual tiles that catch your eye. Working to a colour scheme creates a unified theme, but is not essential. When you have a good collection, including a few plain tiles, arrange them like a patchwork until you are happy with the design and then fix them to the wall.

▼ **Bathtime classics**
It only takes a few large tiles, embossed with scenes from Greek mythology and slotted into a roomfull of marbled tiles, to bring a glamorous touch of luxury to this bathroom. Note how the band of narrow tiles under the rim of the tiled bathside is carried on at the same level around the wall.

Border lines

A narrow border strip is one of the most attractive ways of giving a smart finish to tiling. This can range from a delicate band of fine pattern to a bold, wide frieze. Borders can be added at ceiling or dado level or to round off a partly tiled surface. Running a border or frieze round the room at dado height can help draw together aspects of an awkwardly shaped room, and may give an impression of more pleasing proportions. Tile strips can also be used very effectively to frame attractive features like a pretty mirror or a small window.

Tiles specifically designed as borders are frequently made to complement a whole tiling range. They are usually narrow rectangular half-tiles with flat or raised surfaces. Dado tiles with a raised sill are also available. You could create your own border effects by laying single rows of coloured or patterned tiles round plain ones.

Grouting

For good looks at low cost, consider using coloured grouting with inexpensive plain tiles, to give a very striking fine grid of colour. Grouting can be bought in a range of colours, or you can buy pigment to colour it yourself.

Water is liable to collect on a horizontal worktop, particularly in the grouted strips. Always use waterproof grouting to stop water seeping under the tiles. Also ensure that the grouting fills the gaps between the tiles, to stop crumbs accumulating in crevices.

In time, grouting can get very dirty and needs to be cleaned regularly with a stiff brush and domestic bleach. It may occasionally be necessary to rake out the existing grout and replace it.

Tiling options

Tiles are far too decorative to be restricted to worktops and walls. They can be laid as a waterproof, wipeable lining on kitchen or bathroom shelves and windowsills, or to brighten up window reveals. A series of tiles intended as a mural or wall panel can look equally striking when fixed horizontally on a table-top, a kitchen work surface or beside a wash basin.

As the existing focus of a room, the fireplace is one of the very best places to display beautiful tiles. Use them as panels on either side of the grate and to line the hearth.

Disguising poor tiling

Sometimes when you move house, you inherit a hideous tiled bathroom or kitchen. Unfortunately, tiles can be tricky and costly to remove. A more immediate remedy is to paint over them, using a coat of metal primer before covering them with gloss or eggshell paint in your preferred colour. Another way of disguising unwanted tiles is to stick tile effect panels on top of the original tiles until you can get round to fitting new ones.

▲ **A grate idea**
Decorative tiled panels flanking the grate can turn a fireplace into a stylish showpiece. Here, the Art Nouveau style of the tiles and the fireplace complement each other perfectly. Plain heat-resistant glazed tiles in the hearth are easy to keep spotlessly clean.

Tiling a splashback

Ceramic tiles provide a decorative and practical finish to walls, worktops and fireplaces. The choice is enormous, with a splendid array of colours, shapes and surface textures available – from plain tiles with clear or mottled colours, to charming rustic designs or bold, multi-coloured motifs.

With the ever-increasing range of equipment for home decoration, tiling is now well within most people's capabilities. Careful planning and the use of the right tools will reward you with a highly professional finish.

Choosing the tiles
Tiles are one of the most long-lasting surfaces in the home, so make your choice carefully. Catalogues, magazines and shop displays give ideas on colours and designs. Decide whether you want plain or patterned tiles, or a combination of both. Plain tiles are cheapest, but you can liven them up by adding a few patterned tiles in groups or at random. Border designs and contrast edgings will also add interest to plain tiling, and can be used to pick out the main colours of the room.

The size of tile and its surface texture should also be considered. Most tiles are square, either 110mm (4¼in), 150mm (6in) or 200mm (8in), but the larger 'continental' size of 150 x 200mm (6 x 8in), is being used more and more. Many-sided tiles, curved tiles and mosaics are also available.

Tiles usually have smooth, glossy surface finishes, but for rustic appeal, tiles with an uneven or embossed surface, make unusual alternatives.

▼ **Combining colour and patterns**
White tiles with blue corner details are combined in different ways for a variety of effects. They make a chequerboard when used with plain blue tiles. Used with each other, the corner patterns combine to form circles. The single motifs and border tiles add extra interest.

Measuring up

As ceramic tiles are expensive, it makes sense to measure up accurately. Multiply the height by the width of the area to be covered to find the number of square metres (yards) and divide by the area of one tile to find out how many you need – add at least 10 per cent for breakages.

If combining different tiles or using a border pattern, make sure you buy all the tiles in either metric or imperial measures. Metric and imperial measures will not convert exactly, so if you try to mix them, the tiles will not line up.

Layout

It is usually necessary to cut some of the tiles in order to fit an area exactly. These cut tiles should always be placed at the edges of the tiling, and never in the middle. Since it is difficult to cut thin strips of tile, try to arrange the tiles so that those at the edge are not too narrow.

Preparation

Careful preparation of the walls makes it easier to fix the tiles and prevents problems later on. Strip off any wallpaper, fill cracks and holes with interior filler and remove flaking paint. Sand smooth, then follow up with a coat of stabilizing solution to provide a good surface for the adhesive.

If necessary, it is possible to tile over old tiles provided that they are securely fixed. Clean the old tiles and use a tile cutter to score the surface to give a key for the adhesive. Don't lay individual tiles directly over the old tiles; stagger the starting level so that grout points don't coincide anywhere along the lines of tiling.

Tools

adhesive Choose the right one for the job: thin bed adhesive for smooth, level surfaces; waterproof for bathrooms and showers; heat-resistant for use around cookers and fireplaces; flexible on wooden surfaces that have a tendency towards movement. Five litres (1 gallon) of thin bed adhesive will cover approximately 4.16 sq m (5 sq yd).

trowel or spreader The notched edges apply the adhesive in even ridges. A plastic or metal spreader is often supplied free with the adhesive.

grout As with adhesives, different types are available – buy the waterproof type for showers and splashbacks. There is a special non-toxic version, with added fungicide, which should be used for kitchen worktops. Normally white, grout also comes in several colours. 500g (1 lb) of grout will cover approximately 1.65 sq m (2 sq yd).

grout finisher A special tool or piece of dowel used to press grout firmly into place and give a neat, regular finish.

measuring rod Make your own from a long piece of batten, and mark it off at intervals by the tile depth, allowing for the thickness of the grout between each one.

spirit level Used to ensure a straight line and a **plumb line and bob** to measure the true vertical (see page 21). A spirit level which measures vertical as well as horizontal lines can be used instead, if preferred.

marking tools Chalk, felt pen and ruler.

sponge Use a damp sponge to spread grout over the tiles and into the joints. Quicker for large jobs, is a thin rubber squeegee, with a handle, like the ones used to clean windows.

tile spacers These ensure a regular gap is left between tiles. Accuracy is easier to achieve with 'universal' tiles, made with specially angled edges which, when butted together, leave a gap the correct size for the grout.

batten Use for larger jobs to position and support the tiles on the wall.

hammer and masonry nails To secure the battens to the wall.

tile cutter There are several types, ranging from a simple tile spike to a tool resembling a pair of pliers with a wheel used to score the tile, and jaws that snap the tile on the scored line. For more ambitious projects, it might be worth investing in (or hiring) one of the combination tools, which will measure, score, cut and snap.

tile file To smooth over cut edges; a carborundum stone, file or abrasive strip is the most effective.

tile nibblers These pincers are used to break off small pieces of tile to fit them round awkward shapes.

frame saw Useful for cutting tiles to fit around pipes and switches.

tip

Professional touch
To ensure the tiles are level and to prevent them from slipping down the wall on to the sink, basin or bath, professionals fix a wooden batten to the wall just below the position of the second row of tiles.

It isn't difficult to do this – a few masonry nails or panel pins will secure a thin batten to a plaster wall. The bottom row of tiles is fixed to the wall last, after the batten has been removed.

▶ **Bath surround**
Two rows of tiles round a bath are easy to tile yourself, and provide an attractive and practical finish.

STARTING TO TILE

1 Planning tile positions Place a row of tiles in front of the wall to find the best arrangement. A symmetrical arrangement usually looks best, with cut tiles at each end. However, if tiling round three sides, as round a bath, place a whole tile at each front end, and cut tiles at the back corners.

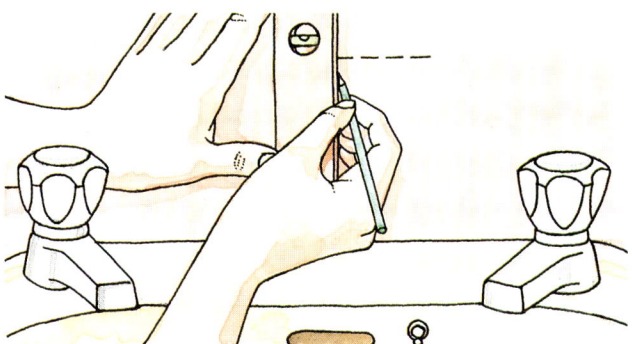

2 Marking the wall Using a plumb line or spirit level, draw a vertical line in the centre of the area to be tiled. Mark where the top of each tile will be to check finished positioning of rows.

For a professional finish, fix a batten below the level of the second row of tiles, using a spirit level to get it straight. Leave the nails sticking out of the batten to make them easier to remove later.

3 Apply the adhesive Using the notched spreader, apply adhesive, working on an area the size of six tiles at a time. Draw the spreader firmly across the wall to get the adhesive even. Do not apply adhesive at the ends of rows where cut tiles will go, and avoid getting any on the batten, if you're using one.

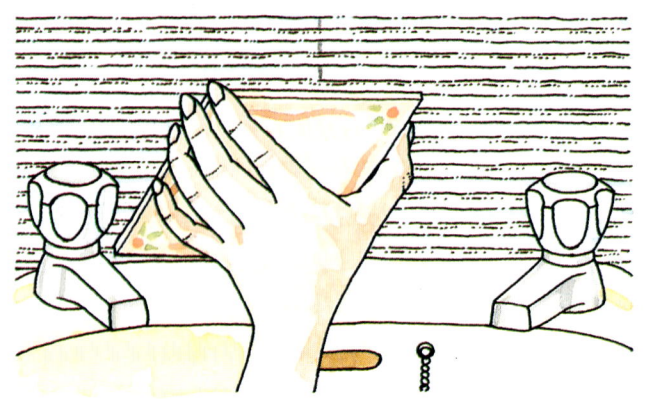

4 Position the first tile Using the basin, bath or batten for support, position the bottom edge of the tile against the wall first, and then press flat. Use the spirit level to check that the tile is horizontal, and adjust slightly if not.

5 Tile the first row Continue laying tiles along the first row. Universal tiles with curved edges can be butted together, but for standard tiles, position tile spacers at upper corners, bedding them down below the level of the tiles so that the grout will cover them. Leave gaps at the ends where tiles need to be cut.

6 Finishing the whole tiles Cover the remaining area with tiles, row by row. Use a spirit level at regular intervals to ensure that the tiles are straight. With a clean sponge, wipe off any excess adhesive from the surface of the tiles.

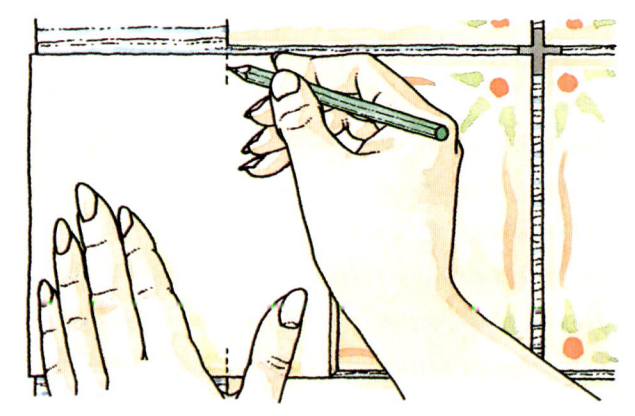

7 Tiling at edges To fill gaps at edges, place a tile in each gap, glazed side down, and mark it at top and bottom with a marker pen; allow space for grouting. On the glazed side, join the marks with the pen and a ruler. Check the tile fits the gap before cutting.

8 Cutting tiles Firmly score once along the marked line using a ruler to guide the blade. Position the jaws of the snapping tool on either side of the marked line and squeeze to make a clean break. Smooth down cut edges with a file before fixing. If a tile only needs to be trimmed, score the tile, then use pliers or nibblers to remove the excess.

9 Leave to set When all the tiles have been laid, wipe them clean and allow 24 hours for the adhesive to set completely. If using a batten, wait until the tiles above it are firmly fixed and the adhesive has set. Then remove the batten and tile the last row. Leave to set.

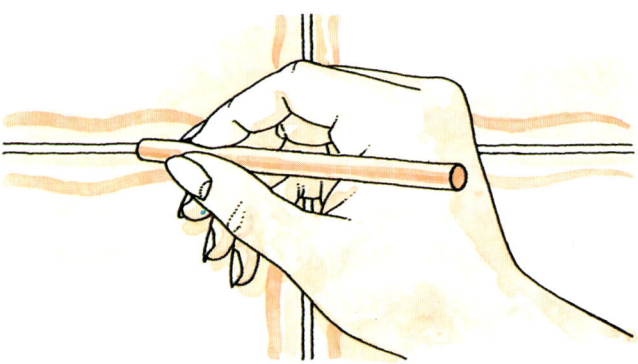

10 Apply grout Mix the grout, according to the instructions and, using a slightly damp sponge or squeegee, spread liberally over the joins between the tiles, forcing the grout into the gaps as you go. Wipe off any excess before it sets. Smooth down the surface with a bit of dowelling or the blunt end of a pencil. Polish with a soft cloth.

11 Apply sealant Use a proprietary sealant or sealing strip instead of grouting where the splashback meets the sink or bath to prevent water penetration. Apply sealant directly from the nozzle of the tube, then smooth with the back of a spoon dipped in water. Remove excess immediately with a damp cloth.

Simple shelving

In any house where space is tight, increasing the amount of storage on offer will help to ease the squeeze. Shelving is the cheapest way to make use of odd corners and unused spaces and requires neither special skills or equipment. Using widely available materials, any competent home decorator can put up a simple shelf with bracket supports.

▼ An extra shelf
This combination shelf and curtain pole is very versatile: the shelf can provide a home for plants and favourite crockery, while the pole, here, is used for drying herbs.

Choosing shelf materials
Select the material for the shelf not just because it looks good but bearing in mind what it is going be used for. Strong materials are needed to take the weight of books, while thin, lightweight shelves are fine for, say, china and ornaments. Any shelf will sag if the distance between the supports is too large, so remember, the thinner the shelf, the shorter the span between the brackets. See the chart overleaf for bracket spacing on solid walls.

Timber There are two types available, either **hardwood**, which is extremely durable, though quite expensive, and softwood, such as pine. Whichever type of wood you choose, specify planed square edge timber (PSE), which is planed on three sides and has a smooth finish that needs little extra work.

Man-made boards These often come veneered with a wood grain and with all four edges finished. If it has to be cut, an edging strip can be ironed on to the exposed side later. If the surface is going to be painted use plywood, blockboard or extra-rigid medium density fibreboard (MDF).

Glass This is ideal for display shelving in an alcove or across a window. The edges should be perfectly smooth for safety. The glass merchant will be able to do this when you buy the shelves.

Choosing brackets

When putting up a small shelf on its own, or perhaps a pair, you can use basic L-shaped brackets.

These vary from simple shaped pieces of wood to fancy wrought iron scrolls. Some shops offer a shelf pack with brackets and fixings included, otherwise you have to buy all the items separately.

Shelf fixings

Masonry walls Brackets are securely fixed with screws and wallplugs. To attach heavy shelves to masonry walls use an expanding wall anchor. This is an all-metal fixing that consists of a bolt with an expanding outer shell that grips the sides of the hole as the bolt is tightened.

Hollow walls If possible, screw directly into the wooden framing uprights that lie behind the wall facing. To locate these, tap the wall with your fingers until the sound is more solid and check it is the right spot by piercing the board with a bradawl. Fix the shelf brackets to these uprights (usually spaced at 40cm (16in) intervals) using wood screws at least 3.8cm (1½in) long. A lightweight shelf which is not expected to take heavy loads can be put up on a hollow wall using special screws which open out behind the wall.

Spacing brackets		
Thickness	19mm (¾in)	2.5cm (1in)
Medium load	70cm (27in)	90cm (36in)
Heavy load	50cm (20in)	70cm (27in)

▲ **On display**
These pine shelves fill the alcove providing useful storage space for many household objects, which look better displayed than hidden away.

◄ **Decorated brackets**
Plaster corbels have been used to support a simple kitchen shelf adding a decorative leaf design on an otherwise plain wall, and enhancing the overall design of the kitchen.

Materials
Shelves and brackets.
Power or hand drill with a set of drill bits.
Spirit level and plumb line.
Screwdriver and bradawl.
A wood saw if the shelves need cutting to size.
Tape measure, pencil and ruler.
Wall fixings, if not supplied with shelf, including the appropriate screws and wallplugs for the type of wall.

tip

Safety check
When hanging shelves, it is vital to ensure you will not be drilling into electric cables or water pipes. Invest in a cable and pipe finder which gives a signal when passing over a pipe or cable.

PUTTING UP BRACKET SHELVES

1 Positioning the brackets Decide where you would like to position the shelf. The brackets should be placed about 50-75cm (20-30in) apart. Hold a bracket up to the spot and mark with a pencil through each screw hole.

2 Drilling the wall Choose a drill bit suitable for the type of wall and one size larger than the screws you plan to use. Hold the drill up to the first pencil mark, keep it at right angles to the wall and use a steady pressure to drill holes to the correct depth (at least 2.5cm (1in) into solid brick). Do not force the drill in or this will make it wander. Insert the wallplugs then screw the bracket into place.

3 Check it is level Hold the second bracket in position against the wall. Place the shelf across the two brackets with the spirit level resting on top. When satisfied that the shelf is straight, mark the screw holes of the second bracket with a pencil.

4 Dealing with longer shelves A centre bracket may be needed to stop a longer shelf from sagging in the middle. Attach the two outside brackets first and place the shelf on them before marking the position of the third bracket.

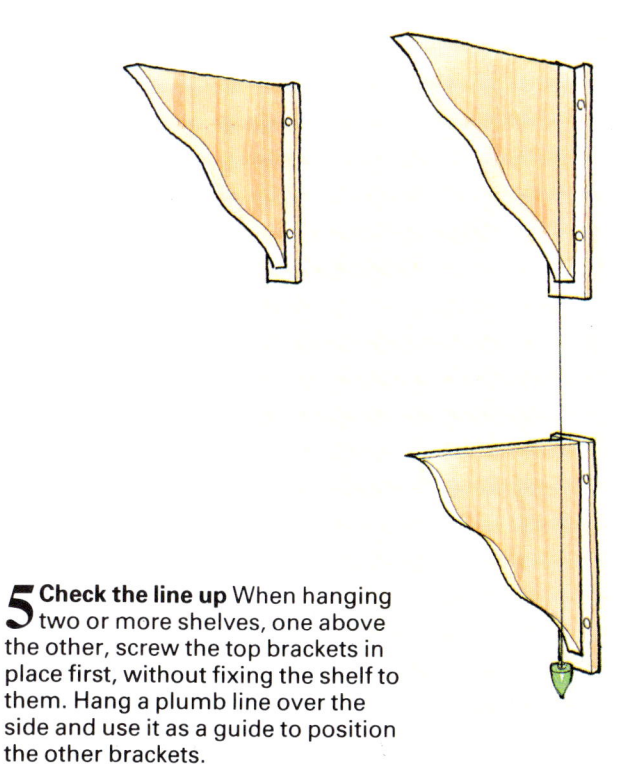

5 Check the line up When hanging two or more shelves, one above the other, screw the top brackets in place first, without fixing the shelf to them. Hang a plumb line over the side and use it as a guide to position the other brackets.

▲ *Homemade brackets* With a little skill, and a mitre box for cutting accurate angles, you can make your own brackets from lengths of timber screwed together.

tip

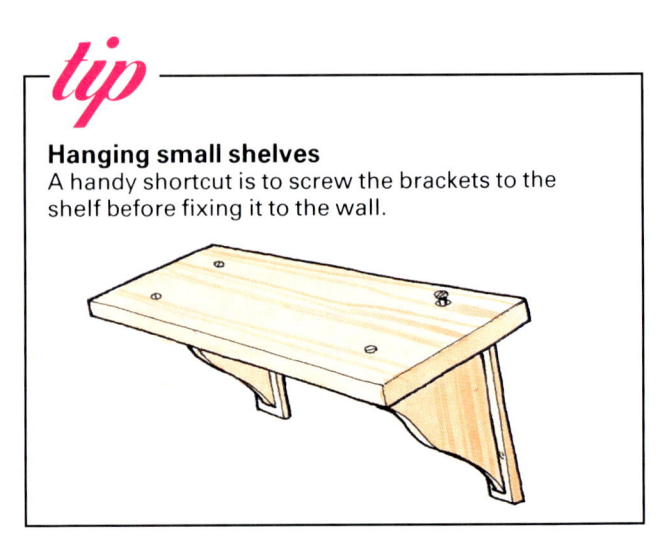

Hanging small shelves
A handy shortcut is to screw the brackets to the shelf before fixing it to the wall.

◀ **Green corner**
A white corner shelf, with unusual brackets holds a white bowl full of trailing plants.

▼ **Lacy detail**
Cast iron shelf brackets have an open lacy effect, which fit in with the cut out detail above the hob.

Cupboard love

As the old proverb says, 'A place for everything and everything in its place' makes for an orderly life. In an ideal world, every item would have a regular home in the house. To ensure this, you need plenty of ever-expanding cupboard space – and a family that puts things back where they belong.

When choosing a cupboard pay attention to the door design. Wood panelled doors will neatly hide the contents from view, no matter how untidily, which is great for the out-of-sight, out-of-mind school of housekeeping. Glass fronts, open metal grilles or chicken wire on the doors create a display cabinet. Behind either sort of doors, there may be shelves, drawers, hooks, pegs or rails.

▼ **Quilt cupboard**
A gracious old cupboard provides an ideal hideaway or display case for some pretty quilts and blankets.

▲ **Fireside recesses**
Building a fitted cupboard with shelves into an alcove beside a chimney breast makes sensible use of a rather inaccessible area of the room. Here, wire mesh instead of door panels protects some handsome, valuable volumes from prying fingers and idle curiosity, but still lets them be seen and admired.

▼ **Part of the scenery**
A run of cupboards along the bedhead wall provides plenty of much-needed storage and hanging space in this bedroom. They have been taken over the bed and become part of the architecture of the room. Some door panels are replaced by mirrors, while fabric behind the glazed doors links with the curtains.

Fitted cupboards

The concept of a fitted kitchen or fitted bedroom, with a built-in assortment of cupboards selected to match your personal taste and specific requirements, is a familiar one. Contrary to popular opinion, fitted furniture has been around a long time, so it is just as appropriate in the traditional, country-style home as the free-standing items. Fitted cupboards are popular because they use space efficiently and give the room a comprehensive, planned look.

Shop round before you make a purchase. There are many different styles and materials, from veneered timber to melamine, in rustic country styles and elegant period designs.

Most self-assembly units can be installed by a competent craftsperson. If you are unsure about your skills, it is worth hiring a carpenter to do the job properly or use the shop's fitters.

Locations

The easiest location for fitting an off-the-peg cupboard system is in a straight run along a wall. Such an ideal situation rarely exists, by the time windows, chimney breasts, doors and radiators are taken into account. You may have to consider a radical solution like moving a radiator, knocking out a chimney breast or blocking a redundant doorway to make room for cupboards.

Alternatively, alcoves provide a neat location for a fitted cupboard. In some cases it is possible to create a cupboard by closing off the recess space with a frame and door. An alcove is usually shallow, so in a bedroom you may need to hang clothes against the wall, rather than along it, since a hanger requires a minimum depth of 56cm (22in).

Kitchen cupboards don't generally need to be as deep as hanging cupboards. They can be fitted with shelves for crockery or foodstuffs or with pegs along the back wall to make a broom cupboard.

For an unusual or awkward location, it is wiser to have a customised cupboard built to fit the space precisely. The oddly shaped area under the stairs can be closed off fairly easily with doors and used for all manner of storage.

Fitting considerations

When planning the location of a cupboard, always allow for the opening swing of the doors, plus space for standing while you open them. Leave a clearance in front of at least twice the width of the doors or on average 90cm (3ft). Check that the door to the room and any open drawers won't block the opening of the cupboard doors either.

A cupboard door should open wide, exposing the entire hanging or shelving space. Sliding doors are a neat solution in a small space, but they can sometimes prevent you from seeing the entire interior at a glance.

Lighting is also important if you are to be able to see what is inside. Opening the cupboard doors can cast the interior into shadow, so you may have to relocate light fittings or fix a light inside.

If a cupboard door has a mirror on the outside or inside, make sure that there is sufficient space for you to see yourself full length, at a distance of about 1½-2m (5-6ft). Mirror-lined doors should open with their backs to the window, so that the light shines on you.

◀ **Sat in the corner**
A pine corner cupboard makes good use of otherwise wasted space by storing some fine china. When open, the doors create a frame.

▼ **Behind closed doors**
A wall of tall, narrow cupboards is a splendid solution for those who hanker after an uncluttered kitchen. The empty space above makes a handy shelf for baskets.

▼ **Bathing belle**
Hung on the bathroom wall, this rustic little cabinet provides compact storage for toiletries. Roughly washed white paint gives it a dreamy, sea-worn quality.

Free-standing cupboards

You may prefer to assemble your kitchen or bedroom furniture piecemeal from a variety of cupboards instead of from a fitted range. This produces an accumulated-over-the-years style of furnishing, which is rich in character.

Free-standing cupboards are often really beautiful, well-made items of furniture. They can be antique and collectable, or contemporary in design. Currently, there is a vogue for siting a bedroom cupboard or wardrobe as major pieces of display furniture in the living room, kitchen or hallway, which can look very exciting and magnificent.

One big advantage of free-standing cupboards over their fitted counterparts is that they can be moved. They can also be taken with you when you move; you won't begrudge spending a fair amount of money on a quality cupboard if you know it is going to stay in the family.

The downside is that separate cupboards do not always make the most efficient use of space. A single wardrobe occupies a certain width and depth, depending on its size, plus equal gaps on either side before the neighbouring piece of furniture can be positioned. There will also often be a dead space between the top of the cupboard and the ceiling. With fitted cupboards you could build in a taller unit, making the room look bigger.

Planning your purchases

A home is very rarely sorted out in one go. In fact most people take about four years before they get things right. You need to live in a place to discover what you really need and want in the way of storage cupboards. Spend time planning your needs – a checklist of your requirements will help to focus your mind. If you are an avid shoe collector, for example, you will need adequate storage for them; a voracious reader requires plenty of bookshelves.

In kitchens

Cupboards, whether ready made, home made, built in or free standing, must suit the goods to be stored in them. In an old-fashioned kitchen, a cupboard can be used for keeping brooms and cleaning equipment, as a larder for dry goods, or simply as a storage cabinet.

If you have a large farmhouse-style kitchen, free-standing cupboards and dressers will look solid and charming. The mellow tones of old pine are always attractive, but staining, woodgraining, stencilling or free-hand painted decorations can be applied to add a splash of colour, disguise the ravages of time, tie the piece in with the decorative scheme

▲ **Hide and seek**
What a difference a coat of paint has made to this small cupboard. The inside glows in a pinkish coral colour and acts as a warm contrast to the cool blue exterior.
   As a result, it has found a delightful new role, displaying a treasure trove of lovely old books and curios. The contents are too interesting to be hidden away, so the doors are left casually ajar and show off the collection.

◀ **Jewel bright**
The current trend for siting bedroom cupboards in the living room is worth copying. This lovely old press has been stained in a brilliant shade of jade, which lends glowing colour and ample storage space to a country-style living room. Treated in this way, it becomes an important decorative feature in the room.

or draw attention to any uniquely fine features.

Old cupboards can be picked up at auctions and house sales for quite reasonable prices, with the best prices being given for the smaller examples which fit most easily into the more confined spaces in contemporary homes. Do check the dimensions of the item before you make a bid, especially if you have a narrow or awkwardly shaped hallway through which you will have to manoeuvre the piece into position.

Some old wardrobes can be so large, in fact, that you may have difficulty in getting it into your home or up the stairs to the bedroom. However, such excellent bargains can be picked up that it might be worth considering carefully dismantling a favourite piece, as long as it is not very valuable, to get it into the room. It can then be reassembled once it is in place.

An attractive cupboard can be a great way of making use of otherwise useless space. In the front hall or lobby, it can be used to store outdoor gear, while a small cupboard on a landing could be useful for storing linen.

▲ **Wired for display**
The beauty of a wire-fronted cupboard is that the interior is always clearly visible yet ventilated, even when the doors are closed. This opens up umpteen opportunities for some zany decorating ideas. For instance, here, potted paper sunflower heads and candles in glasses, stand proudly and somewhat incongruously in front of the more conventional stacks of china plates and tureens.

▶ **Reformed character**
Paint techniques are simple devices for transforming the character of an old cupboard. Here, the pine was treated to give it a softly limed effect.
Originally intended for display, this cupboard has also undergone a change of use and now provides attractive hanging space in a country bedroom.

Decorative finishes

A beautiful old polished mahogany or satinwood cupboard, with a wonderfully rich grain and patina, is a lovely object in its own right and will be a significant feature in any decorative scheme. It only needs to be given plenty of space to be seen to advantage.

Less attractive fitted and unfitted cupboards can be finished in a variety of ways, to fit in amicably with their surroundings. Doors may be solid, glazed or filled with lattice work, metal grilles or chicken wire. You can entirely alter the appearance of a cupboard by changing its doors, replacing plain glazing with coloured glass, or painting the glass to emulate a stained glass panel effect.

Glass doors can be screened with gathered fabric, picked up from other soft-furnishings in the room to provide a visual link. Lace pinned against the glass, showing all the intricacy of the design, also looks remarkably pretty.

Paint finishes

There are a host of attractive paint techniques that can be used to incorporate a fitted cupboard into the overall room scheme, or to give an old or plain cupboard a new lease of life. Graining, dragging and sponging provide you with plenty of opportunities to express your creativity and enhance a rather plain piece of furniture.

Some of the prettiest effects are achieved using bright, unusual colour combinations, combined with distressed paint work. You could simply pick a colour from the decorative scheme and use that or go for a bold contrast colour, so that the cupboard becomes an important colour accent.

Scandinavian designs offer inspiring ideas for painted furniture, in lovely shades of blues and greens gently washed and rubbed to give them a time-worn quality. America, too, has a long tradition of painted furniture; the colourful folksy, naïve designs of the Pennsylvania Dutch are especially jolly, and ideal for a child's room or an old-fashioned country kitchen.

Instead of paint, wallpaper can be pasted into the door panels and varnished, again providing a visual link with the rest of the room. Stencils, freehand painting or découpage techniques can also be applied to create charmingly original effects.

Door furniture is also important. Look for pretty ceramic knobs with a floral motif, plain glass or, better still, coloured glass knobs in brilliant colours. Brass is traditional and adds a touch of mellow sparkle.

▲ **Classical designs**
Imaginative motifs, skilfully painted in a sensitive colour scheme, create a masterpiece of a cupboard.

▼ **Blushing trellis**
A spiralling ribbon motif on the border inspires a bold lattice treatment for these cupboard panels.

Wire-fronted cupboards

Fitting wire mesh instead of glass or wood as the door panel of a cupboard can transform it from a mundane piece of furniture into one with great character or distinction. The outcome depends on the style of wire grille used; while a panel of chicken wire conveys a genuinely rustic feel to the whole room, a finer, patterned brass grille, like those used for radiator covers, imparts an air of sophistication.

Substituting wire mesh for a door panel is an easy project to tackle at home. It also presents a marvellous opportunity to revamp any modest but outmoded cupboard you may have found when rummaging through your garage, attic or local junk stall. While recognizing that the cupboard has potential and is too good to throw away, you know it wouldn't really fit into your current decorating scheme in its present condition. The question is, how do you set about transforming and updating it?

The conversion of a cupboard

When discovered, all dusty and dirty, hidden away in the corner of the garden shed, this cupboard was virtually a plain wooden box that had been home to numerous spiders and flower pots over the years. As luck would have it, its discovery coincided with a plan to redecorate the bathroom in a lively colour scheme of yellow and blue. Since a decision had already been taken to get rid of the old cracked basin and un-box the cast-iron bath, choosing a Victorian style wash bowl to match seemed most appropriate. But it needed a base, which is when the possibility of using the cupboard was raised.

▼ **A starring role**
The cupboard supporting the wash basin was saved from the scrap heap and diligently restored to play a vital role in this stylish bathroom.

Materials

For preparation
Wood filler
Paint or **varnish stripper** and **wood primer**, if necessary

For painting
Glasspaper
Undercoat and **eggshell paint**
Paint brush and **clean cloths**

For the wire front
12mm (½in) gauge **chicken wire**
Lengths of 30 x 6mm (1¼ x ¼in) **lath**
Saw
12mm (½in) **panel pins**
Hammer, pliers and **screwdriver**

For the curtain
Length of **curtain wire**, **cup hooks** and **eyes**
Fabric
Sewing machine and **cotton thread**

For the wash bowl
Jigsaw
Electric drill and **wood bit**, **masonry bit**, **wallplugs** and **woodscrews**
Silicone sealant
Plumbing accessories or a plumber

TRANSFORMING A CUPBOARD

A complete make-over on a small cupboard like this goes through several phases:

PREPARATION

Examine the cupboard for damage, and repair if necessary, before cleaning ready for painting.

1 Looking for damage First examine the cupboard very carefully, inside and out, to make sure it is sound in frame and timber. Any signs of woodworm will need treatment with a proprietary insecticide before taking it indoors.

2 Cleaning it up Stand the cupboard on a dust sheet or newspaper and give it a good brush down, inside and out, to remove all the cobwebs and loose dirt. Then wipe down with a damp cloth.

3 Removing handles and knobs Take out the drawer. Unscrew the cupboard door handle and the drawer knobs. You can replace them after painting, or select others to match the new image of the cupboard and co-ordinate with the rest of the decor.

4 Taking out the front door panel Unscrew the hinges and lift the door off. Remove the pins holding the door panel in position and knock it out lightly with a hammer, working from front to back.

5 Stripping If the paint or varnish surface is in a bad state, use a chemical stripper to remove it and apply primer before painting.

◀ *A magical metamorphosis*
Transforming a plain, dirty wooden cupboard into this attractive vanity unit involves a number of decorating techniques – painting it, fitting a wire front to the cupboard door, making a curtain and, finally, cutting a hole in the top to hold the wash basin.

PAINTING
The cupboard is painted with a two-tone colour-wiped technique to create a streaky appearance.

6 Sanding down If the surface coating is sound, rub over it with a piece of fine glasspaper, to remove any uneven areas of paint or varnish and to key the surface ready for painting. Fill any major dents, cracks or scratches with wood filler at this stage.

7 Putting on the undercoat Select the two shades of paint to match your colour scheme. Apply the paler paint as an undercoat over the whole cupboard, inside and out, on both sides of the door frame and the drawer front. Allow to dry and sand down before painting top coat.

8 Putting on the topcoat Dilute the darker eggshell paint for the topcoat by a third with white spirit to thin it slightly. When the basecoat is thoroughly dry, wipe on a film of topcoat with a clean brush. Then, while it is still wet, wipe off some of the paint with a cloth so that the paler colour below shows through in places. Let the paint dry before assessing the result and touching up, where necessary, to get the effect you want. For a more conventional look, paint on an undiluted topcoat.

9 Finishing the surface Since the cupboard will be standing in a bathroom, rub furniture wax all over the surface with a clean, dry cloth for extra waterproofing and lustre. Buff to a sheen with another soft cotton cloth. Alternatively, apply two coats of satin or matt varnish to protect the surface of the cupboard.

WIRING
Fitting the wire mesh panel in the door is surprisingly easy. A supplier will cut the wire and laths to size.

10 Choosing the wire Pick a fine meshed, 12mm (½in) chicken wire, available from hardware stores. Measure up the dimensions of the front panel and cut out a sheet of chicken wire 12mm (½in) larger all round with a pair of pliers or wire cutters.

11 Fitting the wire in place Cut two lengths of lath to match the width of the door panel. Then, add twice the width of the lath to the height of the door panel and cut two lengths to match this measurement. Check that there is enough clearance for the door to close properly. Lay the door frame face down on a firm, flat surface. Straighten out the chicken wire as far as possible, so that it sits squarely behind the panel hole. Align the laths over the wire edges and fix in place with panel pins.

MAKING THE CURTAIN
The panel behind the wire can be faced with a screen in the same material as the room's blinds. Cut a rectangle of fabric twice the width of the panel by the height plus 10cm (4in) allowance for simple cased headings at both ends. The neatened fabric is then gathered on to a curtain wire threaded through each narrow casing and fixed to the inside of the door, top and bottom, with small hooks and screw eyes.

Replacing the fittings Fit the old or new door and drawer knobs in place. In this case, square off-cuts of planed batten are painted blue to match the rest of the woodwork and tiles in the bathroom. Double-threaded dowel screws are used to fit the knobs in place. Replace the drawer and re-hang the cupboard door.

Note You can stop the restoration of the cupboard at this point and have a presentable little piece of furniture that will fit happily into a bedroom, bathroom or kitchen decor. Or you can proceed to convert it into a fitted stand for a wash bowl.

BASIN AND PLUMBING
The wash bowl is inset through a hole cut in the top of the cupboard. To accommodate the bowl, the base of the drawer is removed while its front is pinned permanently closed. The back and side panels may also need notching around the skirting and pipework to fit the cupboard tightly against the wall. Unless you want to tackle the plumbing, leave the fitting of the taps and waste pipes to a professional plumber.

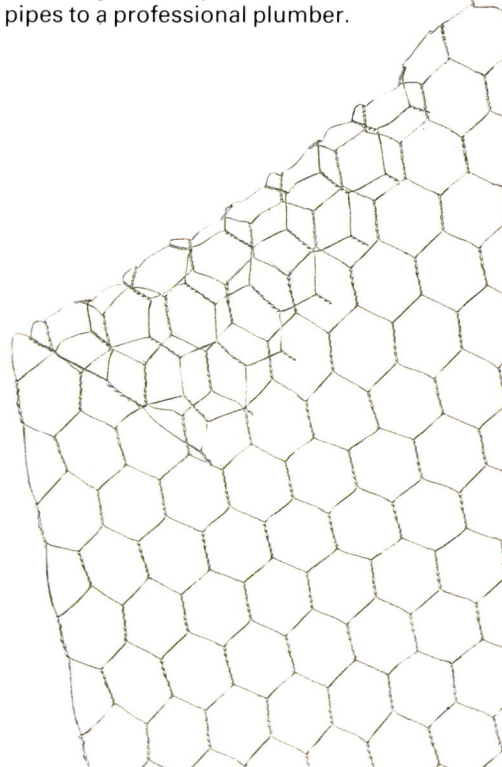

Other mesh-fronted cupboards

Wire-panelled cupboards turn out to be highly adaptable, equally fitted to the informality of a country kitchen or the refinement of a living room. The open wire mesh displays the contents of the cupboard while, at the same time, preventing them from falling out. This system works admirably for securing and exhibiting collections of books and valuable china or glass as well as more everyday items such as a multi-coloured stack of towels. Another advantage is that the cupboards are well ventilated, which means that they stay fresh and can be used to store vegetables and fruit.

Instead of wire mesh, you could install trellis or a more elaborate cut-out metallic or wooden screen in the front panel for another completely different effect. In all cases, you can either leave the mesh open or back it with some material, a piece of lace or a pane of glass. A further variation in which a strong, broad wire mesh is fixed over the front of the cupboard door can also be remarkably striking.

▲ **Wire works**
The contents of this kitchen cupboard are safe yet clearly visible behind wire-fronted doors. Serrated shelf-edgings, cut with pinking-shears, enhance the decorative effect, while sprigs of holly add a dash of festive colour at Christmas time.

◄ **A cage of curios**
A wire-fronted cupboard contributes a casual touch of rustic wit and style to a country living room. Exhibiting quaint collections of china and colourful painted carvings behind the wire mesh increases the curiosity of their appeal as objets d'art.

Introducing lighting

▲ **Night light**
Simplicity is the key to this cosy bedside lighting in a country attic.

Lighting is an important, but often overlooked aspect of the appearance, atmosphere and comfort of any home. With clever lighting a dull room reveals interesting nooks and corners, a cold room becomes warm and inviting, and an awkward workspace is suddenly a pleasure to work in. To understand the importance of artificial light in our lives, imagine the world before electricity when the working day was defined by sunset and sunrise. Everyday activities like cooking and sewing were carried out in poor lighting conditions which made simple tasks difficult and strained the eyes. Candles and later gaslight gave limited illumination and were inflexible compared to the immense range of lighting possibilities today.

Electric light has freed us in a way that is now hard to appreciate. Good task lighting means that we can work comfortably where we want and when we want – you can even work through the night in a windowless basement if it suits you. But where modern lighting really comes into its own is in the creation of atmosphere. As long as you grasp and apply the basic principles, you can, with a little imagination, create a home that is practical, comfortable and individual. Your hall can be warm and welcoming and your living room a soothing retreat in which to relax. In the kitchen you can combine function with friendliness, while your bedroom can be as cosy and romantic as you could wish.

A lighting checklist

In order to analyze the lighting requirements for a particular room, it is helpful to draw up a checklist.

Does the room have one function or several? Many rooms have to be multi-functional; clever lighting can make one room seem like several, illuminating dining, working, reading and sitting areas in different ways.

What mood do you want to create? In a living room you will want a different mood from that in the kitchen or bathroom. Your requirements must be clearly defined in your mind if you are to achieve them.

How many people use the room? Do any of them have special requirements? Children, for instance, may need somewhere for their homework, in which case you will need a good desk light. If you have an elderly member of the family you'll want an easy chair with a cable-switched reading lamp within easy reach beside it.

Is it a child's room? Always use safety plugs, make sure hot bulbs are out of reach and lamps are stable, and avoid trailing cables. Task lighting shouldn't be too bright – 40 or 60 watt bulbs are quite adequate.

Are there practical limitations? The extent to which you can rearrange the lighting in a room depends on how flexible the existing electrical supply is. Are you prepared for the expense and disruption of putting in new wiring and outlets?

What is your budget? If you decide exactly what you are prepared to spend before you start, you won't find the costs running away with you. Even if the ideal solution is beyond your means, with a little ingenuity you can probably find a cheaper alternative.

Types of lighting

General lighting provides background illumination – it gives you sufficient light to see, to find your way around the room, or to watch television. It can come from recessed ceiling lights, pendants or wall lights.

Atmospheric lighting is used to create mood and to add depth and interest to a room. The country style requires soft, indirect lighting, evoking a period feel of flickering fires and candlelight. Soften lighting effects by concealing lights behind pelmets and objects; consider using uplighters and corner and floor lamps for soft effects.

Task lighting allows you to carry out specific activities, for instance spotlights on kitchen work surfaces, standard lamps for reading, adjustable lamps for close up work on hobbies and sewing.

Display lighting allows you to highlight favourite objects. Undershelf strips will show off the contents of a china cabinet; a spotlight can be beamed on to a large house plant.

Halls and porches

A brightly lit porch is a welcome sight when you return home after dark, and you won't have to fumble in the dark for your key. It also allows you to check who your evening visitors are and helps deter potential burglars.

Lighting in the hall is important because it is the first place that visitors see and it sets the tone for the rest of the house. It should be warm and welcoming – so many thoughtfully arranged homes are let down by bleak and functional entrance halls. When lighting the hall, bear in mind that you need to illuminate the stairs properly. Make sure that you can switch hall and landing lights on from both levels.

▲ **Kitchen lights**
Small strip lights cleverly concealed behind the wooden pelmets in these kitchen units provide excellent lighting for the work surfaces.

◀ **Create a mood**
A pendant over your dining table creates a an intimate pool of light over the eating area – and helps to distract the guest's attention from any possible kitchen muddles behind the scenes.

Lighting the country kitchen

In a kitchen good working light is essential for efficiency and safety. Accidents can happen in poorly-lit kitchens. You need good, comfortable overall lighting – because inevitably the family congregates in the kitchen – and bright task lighting over the work surfaces. These can be lit by downlighters or spots which shed a pool of light on to the working surface and should be placed directly above and slightly to the front of the work surface. If you have wall-mounted cupboards use fluorescent or incandescent tubes which can be hidden behind pelmets under the cupboards.

With fluorescent light, choose a colour-corrected tube – the old-fashioned daylight tubes had a chilly bluish cast. Avoid lights with a pinkish cast in a dining or serving area as these can make meat look undercooked.

If you have a combined kitchen and dining room you can't really get away from the cooking clutter while you're eating. One way to overcome this is to have separate lighting systems for the dining and the kitchen areas. A pendant light hung low over the table, or a rise-and-fall fitting, will shed a pool of light on the eating area, making that the centre of attention. By switching off the lights in the working area you can draw attention away from the pots and pans and concentrate on the meal.

Living rooms

The living room is where you entertain and where you relax to talk, watch TV or listen to music. You should try to achieve an adequate level of background lighting, with additional sidelights and display lights to add interest and create a pleasing, homely atmosphere.

General lighting can be provided by recessed downlighters, wall lights, uplighters or a suitable pendant. Choose fittings appropriate to the country look. For walls look at bracket lights in brass with pretty glass shades, wooden brackets with candle-type fittings, or glass uplighters. There is a wonderful range of these, with designs dating from the 1930s and 1940s, and the lights are often cast from their original moulds.

With enough basic lighting you should now create some interest and variety. Look around your room and note its best features and your favourite objects. If, for example, you are lucky enough to have a fireplace with pretty Victorian tiles, you could put a tiny spot light nearby to highlight them. Or you could fill the grate with dried flowers and hide a light behind it.

If you have treasured objects – a collection of glass in a cabinet, a painting

▼ **General and display lighting**
Background lighting for the living room is provided by candle wall-lighters with apple white bulbs to enhance the green tints in the room. The china is highlighted by a spotlight concealed in the cabinet.

▲ **Atmospheric lighting**
A small Tiffany-style table lamp with a tinted apricot white bulb gives a cosy glow to a corner of the living room; consider every available shelf or table as a potential place for soft, indirect lighting.

▲ **Bedroom glow**
Pairs of glass-shaded wall lights on a dimmer switch give a soft romantic feel to the bedroom.

▲ **Light to shave by**
A swan-necked lamp gives a traditional feel to the bathroom and provides good light for the mirror.

▲ **Dressing pretty**
A matching pair of table lamps provides most attractive lighting for a dressing table mirror.

Bathrooms

In bathrooms you need a combination of background lighting and task lighting. Look for fittings which will survive a damp atmosphere – choose plastic and glass shades rather than fabric or paper. A glass pendant bowl will give you a soft diffused light, while a concealed strip or an angle light over the mirror will give you enough light to make-up or shave. Wall lights – either brackets or uplighters – are also very attractive in a bathroom setting.

Bedrooms

Aim for soft background lighting which can be provided by central pendants or wall uplighters. You will also need bedside lights to read by. The switches should be easily accessible even when you are lying down, so that you don't have to fumble in the dark. Ideally, it should be possible to switch on the bedside lamps from the door as well as from the bedside – but this complicated wiring arrangement ought to be carried out by a professional.

Table lamps with fabric shades to match your colour scheme look pretty on bedside cabinets or tables. You will also need specific task lighting – if you have a dressing table, for example, or a long mirror. If your dressing table is in a recess, wall lights may be the answer, otherwise choose a pretty table lamp that matches the bedside lamps.

or a sculpture – arrange your lighting so that they are spotlit in some way. A downlighter, a concealed spotlight or a simple table lamp could all be used to focus attention on the object and allow it to be seen to its best advantage.

Next, turn to practicalities. If children do their homework there you will need a good desk lamp. If one or more people read you should provide adequate lighting of the right type in the right place – a standard lamp behind a chair, or a lamp on a shelf, which sheds light from the side on to the page. If there are hobbyists in the family, they should be catered for – a knitter, for example, should have an adjustable light which shines on to the work.

INDEX

Page numbers in *italic* refer to picture captions

A
Arches, stencilled 18

B
Bathrooms
    lighting 94, *94*
    marble *64*
    panelling *29*
    splashbacks 74-6
    tiles 70-1, *70-1*
    wallpaper borders *24*
    wallpapering *27*
Bedrooms
    cupboards *82, 85*
    decorated floors *47*
    lighting *91*, 94, *94*
    painted *8, 10, 12*
    stained wood *49*
    wallpaper borders *24*
    wallpapered *19*
    wooden floors *33, 44*
Bleaching
    ink marks 60
    wood 55
    wooden floors 46
Borders
    stencilled 15-18
    wallpaper 23-6
Brackets 79
Brushes
    paint 9, 10
    for woodwork 12

C
Chairs, stripping 53-6
Cracks, filling 9
Cupboards 81-6
    finishes 86
    wire-fronted 87-90

D
Dado rails 32
Dents, in furniture 60
Dining areas *35*
    cupboards *86*
    lighting *92*
    wooden floors *43, 44*
Doors
    painting 13
    papering round 28
    panelling round 32
    stained 50
Dust sheets 9
Dyeing, wooden floors 46

E
Eggshell paints 11
Emulsion paints 7
Equipment, woodwork painting 12

F
Fillers, grain 55
Fireplaces 63, *63*
Floors
    stone 61, *61*, 62, *62-3*
    wooden 33-6
    woodstrip *34*, 37-40, *37-40*
Floral patterns
    stencilling *15-18*
    wallpaper 19
    wallpaper borders *23-4*
Furniture
    bleaching ink marks 60
    cleaning 58
    dents, 60
    oiling 60
    removing rings 60
    reviving 57-60
    stained 50
    stripping 53-6
    waxing 60

G
Glass shelving 77
Glasspaper 12
Gloss paint 11
Goggles 9
Grain fillers 55
Grizzled grain *51*
Grouting, bathroom tiles 71

H
Hallways
    lighting 92
    stone floors *61*
    wooden floors *34, 35*

I
Ink marks 60

K
Kitchens
    cupboards *83*, 84-5, *85*, 90
    lighting *92*, 93
    marble surfaces *62*
    painted *7, 11, 13*
    shelving *77-80*
    splashbacks 73-6
    stained wood *50*
    stencilling *52*
    tiles 68, *68-9*

L
Lighting 91-4

M
Marble
    fireplaces *63*
    table-tops *65*
    work-surfaces *62*
Masking tape 9, 12
Matt vinyl paint 7
Mouldings, painting 14

O
Oiled furniture, stripping 54
Outdoor wood stains *51*

P
Paint
    choosing 7
    cleaning up 10, 13
    for woodwork 11
    quantities 7
    stripping 12, 53-6
Paint brushes 9
    using 10
    for woodwork 12
Paint kettles 9
Paint rollers 9
    trays 9
    using 10
Painting
    cupboards 86
    doors 13
    equipment *8*, 9
    mouldings 14
    stone-effects 66
    surface preparation 9
    techniques 7-14
    windows 14
    wooden floors 46
    woodwork 11-14, *11-14*
Panelling
    stained 50
    tongue-and-grove 29-32
Porches, lighting 92

R
Radiators
    paint rollers for 9
    papering round *28*
Rollers, paint 9, 10

S
Sanding, wooden floors 41-4
Satin paints 11
Scrapers 12
Scratches, treating 58-9
Sealing, wooden floors 48
Shelving 77-80
Silk paints 7, 11
Sinks, splashbacks 74-6
Skirtings, stained 50

Slate *61*, *65*
Sockets
   panelling round 32
   papering round *28*
Solid emulsion paint 7
Splashbacks, tiling 73-6
Staining
   wood 49-52
   wooden floors 46
Stains
   applying 51, *52*
   types 50
Stairways, painting *14*
Stencilled borders 15-18
   colour variations 18
   continuous borders *16-17*
   measuring 16
   non-continuous borders *18*
   planning 16
   repeats 18
Stencilled wooden floors 45-8
Step ladders 9
Stone 61-6
   effects 66
Strippers
   gel 54, *54*
   liquid 54, *54*
   paste 54, *54*
Stripping wood 53-6
Surface preparation
   painting 9
   wallpapering 19
   wooden floors 41-4
   woodwork painting 12
Switches
   papering round *28*
   panelling round 32

T
Tiles 67-72
   bathrooms 70-1, *70-1*
   cost 67
   disguising poor 72
   fireplaces *72*
   fitting 69
   kitchens 68
   patterned 67
   splashbacks 73-6
Timber *see* Wood
Tongue-and-groove panelling 29-32
Trays, paint rollers 9

V
Varnish
   applying 56
   coloured 56
   stripping 54
   wooden floors 48
Vinyl paints 7

W
Wallpapering 19-22
   borders 23-6
   measuring up 20
   papering *21-2*
   problems 27-8
   surface preparation 19
Wallpapers
   choosing 19
   quantities 20
   wrinkles 20
Walls
   painting 10
   panelling 29-30
   preparation 9
   shelving 77-80
   stone 63, *63*
Waxed furniture, stripping 54
Waxing, wooden floors 48
Windows
   painting 14
   panelling round 32
   papering round *28*
Wire-fronted cupboards 87-90
Wood
   bleaching 55
   cleaning 58
   grain filling 55
   ink-marks 60
   oiling 60
   painting 11-14, *11-14*
   removing rings 60
   repairing blemishes 58-9
   staining 49-52
   stripping 53-6
   surface preparation 12
   tongue and groove panelling 29-30
   waxing 60
Wooden cupboards 81-6
Wooden floors 33-6
   cleaning woodstrip 40
   decorated 45-8
   laying woodstrip *38-40*
   sanding 41-4
   sealing 44
   stained 50
   woodstrip *34*, 37-40, *37*, *40*
Wooden shelves 77-80
Woodworm, treating 59

Acknowledgements

Photographers: 7 Dulux/Welbeck PR, 8(l) Eaglemoss Publications/John Suett, 8-11 Dulux/Welbeck PR, 12 Sanderson, 13 Magnet, 14 Crown/Charles Barber Lyons, 15 Robert Harding Picture Library, 16 Ametex/Welbeck PR, 17(tl) Ken Kirkwood, 17(tr) Stencil-itis, 18 Ametex/Welbeck PR, 19 Sanderson, 20 Dovedale Fabrics, 23(bl) Sanderson, 23(br) Eaglemoss Publications/Steve Tanner, 24(tr) Ideal Standard, 24(bl) Dorma, 24(br) Sanderson, 26 Forbo Mayfair, 27 Elizabeth Whiting Associates/Di Lewis, 29 Pictures Colour Library, 30 Eaglemoss Publications/Steve Tanner, 32 Jahreszeiten-Verlag/Peter Adams, 33 Robert Harding Picture Library, 34(t) Ronseal, 34(b) Conran Octopus/Simon Brown-de Blacam & Megher, 35(t) Elizabeth Whiting Associates, 35(b) Cuprinol, 36(l) Elizabeth Whiting Associates/Michael Nicholson, 36(r) Cuprinol, 37-40 Junckers, 41 Ken Kirkwood, 42 Eaglemoss Publications/Sue Atkinson, 43 Elizabeth Whiting Associates/Rodney Hyett, 44(t) Crown Paints, 44(b) VPM Redaktionsservice, 45 Elizabeth Whiting Associates/Aprahamian, 46 Jon Bouchier, 47(t) Sanderson, 47(b), 48(t) Cuprinol, 48(b) Maison Marie Claire/Eriaud-Comte, 49-50 Ronseal, 51(t) Modes et Travaux, 51(c,br) Maison Marie Claire/Eriaud-Job, 51(bl), 52 Ronseal, 53(bl) Eaglemoss Publications/Steve Tanner, 53(r) Insight/Michelle Garrett, 56 Ronseal, 57, 59 Colron, 61 Arcaid/Julie Phipps, 62(tl) Smallbone of Devizes, 62(b) Elizabeth Whiting Associates/Rodney Hyett, 62-63(tc) IPC Magazines/Robert Harding Picture Library, 63(b) Arcaid/Richard Bryant, 64(t) IPC Magazines/Robert Harding Picture Library, 64(b) Magnet, 65(t) Habitat, 65(b) Elizabeth Whiting Associates/Rodney Hyett, 66(t) Elizabeth Whiting Associates/Ed Ironside, 66(b) Elizabeth Whiting Associates/Di Lewis, 67 IPC Magazines/Robert Harding Picture Library, 68(t) Elizabeth Whiting Associates/Neil Lorimer, 68(b) Elizabeth Whiting Associates/Brian Harrison, 69(t,bl) IPC Magazines/Robert Harding Picture Library, 69(br) Eaglemoss Publications/Graham Rae, 70(t,br) Cristal, 70(bl) Eaglemoss Publications/Graham Rae, 71(t) Elizabeth Whiting Associates/Tim Beddow, 71(b) Cristal, 72 Stovax, 73 Cristal/Charles Barber Lyons, 74 Tif Hunter, 75 Ken Kirkwood, 77 Elizabeth Whiting Associates/Andreas von Einseidel, 78(t) B&Q DIY Supercentres, 78(b) Houses & Interiors, 79 Dulux/Welbeck PR, 80(tl) Boys Syndication, 80(b) Smallbones of Devizes, 81 Ariadne Holland, 82(t) IPC Magazines/Robert Harding Picture Library, 82(b) Sharps Bedrooms, 83(t) Houses & Interiors, 83(bl) Habitat, 83(br) Elizabeth Whiting Associates/Rodney Hyett, 84(t) Elizabeth Whiting Associates/Andreas von Einsiedel, 84(b) Grange Furniture, 85(t) Ariadne Holland, 85(b) Elizabeth Whiting Associates/Spike Powell, 86(t) Elizabeth Whiting Associates/Peter Woloszynski, 86(b) Elizabeth Whiting Associates/Kudos-Brian Harrison, 87, 88 Anna French, 89 Eaglemoss Publications/John Suett, 90(b) Derwent Upholstery, 90(t) Smallbones of Devizes, 91, 92(cr) Elizabeth Whiting Associates/Spike Powell, 92(bl) Maison Marie Claire/Sarramon-de Roquette, 93 Mazda, 94(tl) Crown Paints, 94(tr) Elizabeth Whiting Associates/Spike Powell, 94(bl) Elizabeth Whiting Associates/Ed Ironside.